IN FLAMING LETTERS

The Black Soldier in War and Society
New Narratives and Critical Perspectives

———————

LE'TRICE DONALDSON AND GEORGE WHITE JR., EDITORS

In Flaming Letters

Lucia Pitts, Poet of the Six Triple Eight

Edited by Verner D. Mitchell and Cynthia Davis

UNIVERSITY OF VIRGINIA PRESS
Charlottesville and London

The University of Virginia Press is situated on the traditional lands of the Monacan Nation, and the Commonwealth of Virginia was and is home to many other Indigenous people. We pay our respect to all of them, past and present. We also honor the enslaved African and African American people who built the University of Virginia, and we recognize their descendants. We commit to fostering voices from these communities through our publications and to deepening our collective understanding of their histories and contributions.

University of Virginia Press
© 2025 by the Rector and Visitors of the University of Virginia
All rights reserved
Printed in the United States of America on acid-free paper

First published 2025

1 3 5 7 9 8 6 4 2

LIBRARY OF CONGRESS CATALOGING-IN-PUBLICATION DATA

Names: Pitts, Lucia M., author | Mitchell, Verner D., editor | Davis, Cynthia J., editor
Title: In flaming letters : Lucia Pitts, poet of the Six Triple Eight / edited by Verner D. Mitchell and Cynthia Davis.
Other titles: Pitts, Lucia M. One negro WAC's story. English
Description: Charlottesville : University of Virginia Press, 2025. | Series: The Black soldier in war and society | Includes bibliographical references and index.
Identifiers: LCCN 2025032531 (print) | LCCN 2025032532 (ebook) | ISBN 9780813954059 (hardback) | ISBN 9780813954066 (paperback) | ISBN 9780813954073 (ebook)
Subjects: LCSH: Pitts, Lucia M. | United States.—Armed Forces—Women—Biography | African American women—Biography | BISAC: HISTORY / African American & Black | HISTORY / Wars & Conflicts / World War II / General | LCGFT: Poetry | Autobiographies
Classification: LCC ML318.C657 N45 2025 (print) | LCC ML318.C657 (ebook)
LC record available at https://lccn.loc.gov/2025032531
LC ebook record available at https://lccn.loc.gov/2025032532

Cover art: Members of the Six Triple Eight during World War II. (Department of Defense)
Cover design: Kelley Galbreath

TO THE MEMORY OF LUCIA M. PITTS

And for our mothers,
The Late Mary Frances Delaney Mitchell
The Late Mary Elizabeth Carroll Davis

CONTENTS

Acknowledgments	*xi*
Lucia Pitts: Her Life and Work	1
Verner D. Mitchell and Cynthia Davis	
One Negro WAC's Story	61
Selected Poems	89
War and the Military	89
Brown Moon	89
A WAC Speaks to a Soldier	92
Let Them Come to Us	94
This Is the Thing We Ask	97
Franklin Delano Roosevelt	99
Little Café	100
Farewell	101
Nature	101
To My Flowers	101
Fallen Castles	102
A Lonely Soul	103
Clouds	104
Sky Dreams	105
Daisies	106

Day of Rain	107
And We, We Fain Would Leave It All Behind	108
Forest at Dusk	108
City Streets on a Rainy Day	109
Dream of Lavation	110
Afternoon Off	110

Love and Romance — 111

To an Admirer	111
I Shall Come to Thee	112
All That I Ask	112
A Flash	113
Lines to a Certain Street	113
That Which Endures	114
If	114
Brief Song	115
Song	115
And Yet	116
Melody	117
Ways	118
Answering the Bubbles	118
Confession	119
Imagery	120
I Was Thinking of You	120
Beloved	121
So You Have Come Back Again	122
Daring Me to Forget	123
Isn't It Strange?	123
I Went Back Over Old Things	124
I'll Sing My Songs	125
La Callada Voz	126
Pagan	126
To One Who Stayed but a Brief While	127
This I Say	128
Sonnet	129
Dark Tender Eyes	129
I Question	130
The First Kiss	131

Challenge	132
Between Ourselves	132
Come Down, Stars	133
Moment in Paradise	134
Promise	135
Requiem	138
If Ever You Should Walk Away	138
One April	139
Bury the Dead	139
Let the Book Close	140
Transient	141
One Day	141
Strange Ways	142
I Offer You Wine	143
Once Upon a Time	143
Friendship	**144**
Satisfaction	144
Friendship	145
Letters	146
To an Exuberant One	147
Fly the Wide Sky	148
Cockeyed Optimist	149
The Circle of Life	**150**
Arrival	150
Similes	151
Birthdays	152
Dirge	152
I Have Heard Songs	153
Nil Sacre	154
This Is My Vow	155
From the Heart	156
Weeds in My Garden	158
And Now Irrevocably	159
Never, Never, Never	160
Time	161
No Time for Tears	162

Art	163
To Lights and Shadows	163
Decision	164
Something of Beauty	165
That Lady Called Lou	166
Warwick Castle	166
Poets	167
Punctuation Suite (Eleven Parts)	167
Capitals	168
Exclamation Mark	168
Dash	169
Question Mark	170
Italics	171
Colon	172
Quotation Marks	173
Semi-Colon	173
Comma	174
Apostrophe	174
Period	175
Appendix: Family Trees	*177*
Selected Bibliography	*181*
Index	*183*

Illustrations follow p. 88

ACKNOWLEDGMENTS

About her colleagues in the Civil Service, Lucia Pitts remarked, "It has always been my feeling that not nearly enough credit is ever given... [to] those who came in during the early days... who had to strive so hard for perfection and be the examples, and who did so much to make it possible for Negroes coming later to find work with Uncle Sam." With her example as guide, we wish to thank many special people who contributed to the publication of this book. Lucia Pitts's maternal descendant, the attorney Jack Drewry, shared his personal memories of Lucia and offered great tidbits of information on the family. Our "fairy godmother," the historian and legal specialist Susan Salus, enthusiastically contributed early newspaper articles, census records, and archival photographs. Our dear Perida A. Mitchell, genealogist extraordinaire, helped construct the Pitts-Harris family tree. Our longtime friends, attorneys Lee and Leandrea Barnhill, were gracious hosts during a research trip to Washington, DC. Dr. Harrison Graves, Loyola University Chicago, graciously agreed to a guided tour of Chicago's historic Bronzeville community. Finally, photographer Daniel Glenn Morris helped restore many early photographs.

The unsung heroes of academic research are, of course, librarians, and we were fortunate in working with some of the very best. Archivists Mackenzie Snare, at the National Afro-American Museum and Cultural Center, Wilberforce, Ohio; Katy Sternberger, of the Portsmouth

Athenaeum, Portsmouth, New Hampshire; Oyinda Omoloja of Afro Charities in Baltimore, Maryland; and Justin Clark, of the Indiana State Library, provided vintage photographs of Pitts's Army unit, the 6888th Central Postal Directory Battalion. In Illinois, Beth Loch, archivist at the Chicago Public Library, provided one of Pitts's essays, while Susan Holderread, archivist at New Trier High School in Winnetka, Illinois, provided a copy of the school's 1920 yearbook containing Lucia Pitts's senior portrait. Robyn Lewis of the San Jacinto College Library and Sofiya Dahman of the University of Memphis Library helped us to acquire rare and out-of-print materials through Interlibrary Loan. We are also indebted to Washington, DC, attorney Barbara Corprew for providing a copy of Lucia Pitts's All Souls Unitarian Church Membership Card.

We also thank our "academic families," especially Professor Yvonne Davis Frear, History chair at San Jacinto College, and Dr. Terrence Tucker, English chair at the University of Memphis. Without their support and encouragement, we could not have presented our work at academic conferences or traveled to the archives, libraries, and interviews that provided us with primary sources.

Academic writing and research can sometimes be a lonely process. We are enormously indebted to friends and colleagues in African American Studies and Literature who kindly offered their time and attention to our project. For their kindness and support of our work, we thank Dr. Louis Henry Gates of Harvard University, Dr. Jennifer James of George Washington University, Dr. Bob Coleman, editor of *Studies in American Culture* at the University of South Alabama, Dr. Laura Vrana of the University of South Alabama, Dr. Sharon Lynette Jones at Ball State University, Dr. Trudier Harris of the University of Alabama, Dr. Jervette Ward of the City College of New York, Dr. LaToya Jefferson-James at Rust College, Professor John M. Lewis of Texas A&M University, and Dr. Loretta McBride at Southwest Tennessee Community College.

A special thank you goes to Drs. Steven Trout and Delia Steverson at the University of Alabama for encouraging us to pursue publication. We first spoke on Lucia Pitts at a University of Alabama English Department Symposium, titled "Cultural Representations of African American War

Experience." Thanks to Julia Wall and Jamie Ryan for organizing such a wonderful interdisciplinary conference.

This book would not exist without the editors at the University of Virginia Press. We are deeply grateful to Dr. Nadine Zimmerli, our sponsoring editor; Wren Morgan Myers, our project editor; and Leslie Tingle, our copy editor, for their constant support, consummate professionalism, and commitment to African American studies, as manifested in the important series, The Black Soldier in War and Society. Our series editors, Dr. Le'Trice Donaldson of Auburn University and Dr. george white jr., of the City University of New York, believed in the project from the very beginning and offered social media savvy, enthusiasm, and wise counsel.

Finally, for their inspiration and many acts of kindness, we thank our families and friends, most especially our children and their descendants, Jared, Courtney, Caring, Milani, Renee, Matthew, Dylan, Jack, Caroline, Sofia, Cecilia, and Annabelle; and, as always, Veronica and Robert, to whom this book is offered with love.

IN FLAMING LETTERS

Lucia Pitts

HER LIFE AND WORK
Verner D. Mitchell and Cynthia Davis

> The history of the Negro in the United States is being written in flaming letters.
> —Lucia M. Pitts, *The Little Fire and How It Grew*, 1963

> A soft light on the darkness,
> Dim shadows on the light;
> A softening of sharpness—
> The reader's great delight—
> —Lucia M. Pitts, "To Lights and Shadows," 1927

When Lucia M. Pitts published her work in the popular poetry column "Lights and Shadows" in the *Chicago Defender* in the mid-1920s, she probably did not anticipate the ways in which her poetry would illuminate her future service in the 6888th Battalion of the Women's Army Corps (WAC) and her stellar career as an administrator and advocate for African American women in the federal government. When her first poems appeared, a reader wrote to Robert S. Abbott, the editor of the *Chicago Defender:* "We have always given Mr. Abbott credit for knowing when he had a good find, and [Lucia Pitts is] 'it' in the fullest sense."[1] By 1919, Abbott had built the *Defender* into the nation's most widely read Black newspaper; the paper reached approximately 600,000 people weekly, two thirds of them outside Chicago.[2] Abbott used the paper to encourage the migration of Blacks from the South to the North, to protest lynchings and other acts of racial violence, and to campaign against segregation in the armed forces and in the South. However, the poetry column "Lights and Shadows," often abbreviated LAS, was among its most popular features. Readers and contributors to the column shared a strong identity and dubbed themselves "LASers."[3] Lucia M. Pitts, a frequent contributor, served briefly as the column's editor. Her 1927 verse "To Lights and Shadows" is both a paean to the column and a prescient introduction to her life and values.

Scholars have begun to recover and revitalize the lives and work of underappreciated twentieth-century African American poets. Gwendolyn Bennett, Waring Cuney, and Helene Johnson have received considerable attention, yet their talented contemporary Lucia M. Pitts (1904–73) remains largely ignored. Like Bennett, Cuney, and Johnson, all of whom continued to write long after the Harlem Renaissance and well into the civil rights and Black Arts movements, Pitts is difficult to label or categorize: a poet, a World War II veteran, and a career administrator, she was a self-described "racial guinea pig,"[4] who took seriously her obligation to uplift the race and open doors for others. She was a member of President Franklin Roosevelt's "Black Cabinet" and the first African American woman employed in several high-profile government jobs, including at the War Department. Despite her illustrious career, however, Pitts kept a low profile; she knew everyone in the Chicago and Harlem Renaissances, but she eschewed a flamboyant lifestyle and avoided the media scrutiny lavished on contemporaries like glamorous chanteuse Nora Holt, blueswoman Bessie Smith, or iconoclastic writer Wallace Thurman. Nor, like her friend Langston Hughes, was she a prolific correspondent; instead, Lucia Pitts was a private individual. She preferred her family and a small circle of close friends and lovers about whose identities she was always discreet.

Given the gaps in the narrative, information on Pitts must be gleaned from widely diffused sources, including newspapers, magazines, government documents, school and military records, census reports, and memoirs by friends and colleagues. Although Pitts's military service was a major influence on her life, the purpose of this book is not to render a corrective to the history of the Women's Army Corps in World War II.[5] Rather, as literary scholars, we adopt an interdisciplinary approach to reconstructing Pitts's life and oeuvre. In interrogating the poetry and nonfiction through a biocritical and literary perspective, our goal is to show how Pitts's voice complicates and expands the lens through which one approaches Black women's agency, subjectivity, and creativity. As historian Samantha Ege states about Pitts's fellow Chicagoan Nora Holt, Pitts "helped expand what was possible for Black women of her time.... [Thus,] telling her story means not tying her contradictory strands onto a neat bow, but embracing the multiple textures and tensions that shaped her life."[6]

In introducing readers to Pitts's life and writing, we seek to illuminate the aesthetic, social, familial, political, and military influences on her work, with a particular focus on her army service with the 6888th Battalion. We argue that Pitts's writing is shaped by her challenging but ultimately life-affirming experiences as a trailblazer who defied the prevailing cultural, racial, economic, and geographic restrictions on African American women. For example, in 1943, Pitts gave up a secure position with the federal government, rejected the counsel of family and colleagues, and joined the army. In 1954, at the age of fifty, Pitts took a solo, thirty-day road trip from Washington, DC, through the segregated South, to California and back. She then shared her adventures in a lively article in the *Washington Afro-American* newspaper. Nothing stopped Lucia Pitts from pursuing her dreams or encouraging others to follow theirs. We conclude this book with one hundred of Pitts's best poems, most collected for the first time, which illuminate the life of this intrepid and talented woman.

Born in Tennessee in 1904 and nurtured by a protective, extended family in Chicago's Bronzeville neighborhood, Pitts grew into an intelligent, vivacious, attractive, and self-confident woman. An adventurous traveler, she lived and worked throughout the United States, including stints in Springfield, Illinois; Tuskegee, Alabama; New York City; Washington, DC; Fort Huachuca, Arizona; and Los Angeles. A highlight of her career, described in a memoir included in this volume, was her service with the US Army in England and France. Although she always held full-time administrative jobs, poetry was her passion. She published her early poems in the *Chicago Defender* newspaper; later, during her European travels, she wrote about the English countryside, Warwick Castle, and Parisian monuments and cafés.[7]

Pitts's greatest accomplishment, however, is found in her strikingly frank and honest love poems. These poems place her in conversation with modernist contemporaries like Edna St. Vincent Millay, with Chicago blueswomen Gertrude "Ma" Rainey and Bessie Smith, and with jazz chanteuse Nora Holt. In Pitts's work, as in that of Millay, Rainey, Smith, and Holt, the female speaker "represents herself as . . . subservient to male desire [but] simultaneously express[es] autonomous desire" and rejects "psychic despair."[8]

Lucia M. Pitts was a versatile writer. In addition to poems and short stories, she penned articles for the African American press; training and education materials for the federal government; a memoir of her military service; and a three-hundred-page autobiography, *The Little Fire and How It Grew,* which describes her battles for civil rights within the federal government. Although her poetry was well-known thanks to the African American press, she did not travel in literary circles. Unlike Langston Hughes, Pitts never benefitted from the patronage of powerful and influential literary figures like Carl Van Vechten, Vachel Lindsay, and Blanche Knopf; otherwise, she would certainly have received the acclaim that eluded her.

In her work Pitts celebrates both the joys and heartbreaks of Black life; however, she firmly rejects the determinism with which some writers in the 1930s and 40s had portrayed the race: as passive victims of racist ideologies and pathological case studies. In this regard, most scholars place her adjacent to her friend Gwendolyn Brooks in the literary canon, and her poetry is often compared to Brooks's work in terms of style and subject. Like Pitts, Brooks had accompanied her family to Chicago's Bronzeville as part of the Great Migration.

Gwendolyn Brooks was from Kansas and Lucia Pitts from Tennessee, but both came of age on Chicago's famous South Side. After high school,

Pitts studied business at the Chicago Commercial Institute,[9] while Brooks majored in English at Woodrow Wilson Junior College. The Commercial Institute was located across from Dunbar Park on 31st and Indiana, in the heart of Bronzeville, an African American commercial and residential neighborhood that rivaled New York's Harlem and Boston's Roxbury; Brooks celebrated the neighborhood in her first poetry collection, *A Street in Bronzeville* (1945).

Given their addresses in Bronzeville, both Pitts and Brooks should have enrolled in Wendell Phillips, Chicago's oldest African American high school. Opened in 1904 in what was a prosperous white neighborhood, by the 1920s Wendell Phillips High was predominantly Black, a result of white flight spurred by the Great Migration. The historian John Burger notes that "part of the reason African Americans settled in Chicago's black belt was that Chicago had a reputation as a good place to live and was known as a place for opportunity and freedom."[10] Phillips High appealed to ambitious, upwardly mobile families and offered a robust college preparatory track. Phillips alum Alonzo Parham recalls that in 1925, in seventh grade, he studied history, English, grammar, physiology, algebra, and French.[11]

Gwendolyn Brooks did attend Wendell Phillips High School, but Lucia followed a different track. Her mother, Janie Harris Pitts, worked as a housekeeper for a family in Glencoe, a village in New Trier Township on the affluent North Shore. Because Janie and Lucia boarded in a home in New Trier, Lucia was eligible to attend New Trier High School, from whence she graduated in 1920. Janie Harris Pitts was clearly intentional in moving to the North Shore and assuring her daughter one of the best high school educations in the country. Lucia recalls New Trier as one of America's most progressive and top-performing schools; she enrolled in the academic track and, importantly, was introduced to poetry.

The Canadian writer and historian Mary Quayle Innis (1899–1972) attended New Trier High a few years ahead of Lucia; according to Quayle Innis, the school's rigorous intellectual atmosphere and the well-equipped facilities, including a library, art room, auditorium, and music program, were unparalleled. New Trier emphasized literature and writing; the canonical writers were studied and prizes awarded for excellence in composition.[12] In terms of poetic themes and metrics, Pitts's reliance on the "greats of the canon," to whom she was introduced at New Trier High School, is clear in these early efforts.

Lucia excelled academically, but she was not particularly happy at New Trier. The student body was overwhelmingly white; she and Hilda Vivien Gordon were in the minority as African Americans, and Lucia endured many "racial hurts."[13] In fact, Lucia's experiences recall those of her friend, the writer Dorothy West, at Boston's prestigious Girls' Latin School; when Dorothy's classmates snubbed her on the street, her mother reminded her that she was at Girls' Latin to get the best education possible and not to make friends.[14] Janie Pitts probably gave Lucia similar advice and encouraged her to participate in Bronzeville's vibrant cultural milieu. A key element in the city's African American culture was the *Chicago Defender* newspaper. Both Gwendolyn Brooks and Lucia Pitts published their early poems in the *Defender*.

There is no question that a major influence on Pitts's poetry was *Poetry*, the modernist, Chicago-based literary magazine founded by Harriet Monroe in 1912. Lucia would certainly have found the magazine in the library of a progressive, literature-focused school like New Trier. In the magazine she would have discovered the work of Edna St. Vincent Millay, Carl Sandburg, Ezra Pound, D. H. Lawrence, Witter Bynner, and Robert Frost. T. S. Eliot's poem "The Love Song of J. Alfred Prufrock" first appeared in the magazine in June 1915.

In 1921, as Pitts began to think of publishing her own work, issues of *Poetry* featured Amy Lowell (June); Rainer Maria Rilke (September); and Wallace Stevens (October). Although Harriet Monroe's own poems tended toward conventional nineteenth-century themes and forms, her editorial taste was eclectic and international; special issues in 1919 featured postwar poetry (July) and the Italian futurist poets (January). In the "News Notes" column for August 1927, Monroe remarks: "This issue is somewhat cosmopolitan. . . . England is represented by three poets, Canada by one, black Africa by one."[15] The African contribution was by Monroe's South African protégé Santie Sabalala, whose poem "The Raid" celebrates Zulu warrior culture. Monroe was not the only one fascinated by the debonair Sabalala: Lucia would be romantically involved with him around the time that Monroe published his work. Yet another issue of *Poetry* featured a sequence of poems about Russia by Lola Ridge, the feminist-Marxist writer who contributed frequently to *New Masses* magazine. Monroe was probably the first to publish in English the Chinese poets Li Po and Wang Wei, as translated by Witter Bynner.

Like her close friends the poet-translator Witter Bynner and the poet-editor Idella Purnell, Harriet Monroe sought out underrepresented voices. Bynner, a champion of African American writers and a judge for the *Opportunity* magazine writing prizes, had established, in conjunction with Purcell's poetry magazine *Palms*, a prize for Undergraduate Excellence in Poetry. The first recipients included Countee Cullen in 1925 and Langston Hughes the following year. In 1926, when Lucia first published in the *Chicago Defender*, the November issue of *Poetry* featured works by Cullen and Hughes. Pitts would certainly have appreciated the fact that, rather than lumping the African American poets together, Monroe carefully contrasted Cullen's formal sonnets with Hughes's blues lyrics, thus exposing readers to the complexity and breadth of Black poetry.[16]

Of course, Pitts had probably already read Hughes's poem "The Negro Speaks of Rivers" in *The Crisis* magazine in 1921, and she would have known that he won first prize in *Opportunity* magazine in 1925 for "The Weary Blues." As literate, cultured, civically minded individuals devoted to racial uplift, the Pitts family would certainly have subscribed to both *The Crisis* and *Opportunity*. In Lucia's formative years, she was thus exposed not only to the very best American writing, but specifically to African American writers who were making their voices heard in mainstream publications.

In addition to *Poetry* magazine and the work of Hughes and Cullen, Pitts looked to several other important sources for her work. Most critics agree that Pitts's most original and innovative poems are her love poems. They were her own favorites, and many of her lyrics, including "Challenge," "To an Admirer," and "Confession," are strikingly frank and technically sophisticated. In this regard, the poet who most influenced her work is arguably Edna St. Vincent Millay. Monroe was the first to publish Millay's "Recuerdo" in 1919, when Lucia was fifteen. The poem's iconic lines about the Staten Island Ferry ("We were very tired, we were very merry / We had gone back and forth all night on the ferry") claim the female speaker's complete freedom, independence, and mobility, and express a sly, irreverent take on women's sexuality. Lucia would later employ similar tones and themes in her own love poetry.

Another influence on Pitts's love poetry is indubitably the lyrics of blueswomen like Ma Rainey and Bessie Smith, both of whom lived in Chicago during Lucia's formative years. Lucia had been exposed to the blues since childhood; her brother Harrison composed blues tunes and worked in Memphis with W. C. Handy. Later, with his two brothers, Harrison operated three Bronzeville taverns that featured popular blues performers. Lucia herself, although she never aspired to a musical career, formed a singing group with four other women and arranged much of their repertoire. The Harmony Quartet performed at community events in Bronzeville. (Though there were five members, they used the name "Quartet.")

Given the respectable status of the Pitts family and their involvement in the church, the Quartet's repertoire was probably more akin to that of Nora Holt, a classically trained pianist, a staunch promoter of the spirituals, and the first music critic for the *Chicago Defender*, than to the raunchy blues of Rainey and Smith. As a major luminary in the Bronzeville cultural scene, Holt was undoubtedly a role model for Lucia. The young poet certainly knew *Music and Poetry*, the magazine Holt started in 1921, as it combined her two major interests. In the magazine, Holt "was keen to explore the possibility of assimilating European and African American musical forms."[17] She emphasized the importance of Blacks "assimilating rather than being assimilated into white culture, thereby suggesting a relationship of reciprocity rather than hierarchy."[18] Pitts would also have read Holt's articles in the *Defender*, in which Holt was an indefatigable booster of African American music as performed in Bronzeville churches and community events, as well as in mainstream venues. Holt, in her varied career trajectory, rejected racial, cultural, gendered, and geographic boundaries, as Pitts would do some years later. Despite the fact that she held a master's degree in music, had composed over two hundred classical pieces, and had cofounded the National Association of Negro Musicians (NANM) in 1919, Holt transitioned from classical music to international acclaim for her sultry and sophisticated blues. She reinvented herself as a cabaret performer, appeared in Paris and New York, dubbed herself "naughty little Nora," and, dressed in glittering gowns, performed a repertoire of erotic suggestion and double entendre.[19]

Like Holt in her cabaret performances, Lucia employed sophisticated diction, grammar, and vocabulary in her poetry. She eschewed the vernacular of the blues; however, the voice, themes, narrative arcs, and philosophy of her poems suggest that she listened to the Chicago blueswomen. In "Challenge," for example, the speaker disparages her admirer's restraint and tenderness and demands a bolder, more physical lover to quench her "raging flame." Bessie Smith expresses a similar idea: "I need a little sugar in my bowl / I need a little hot dog on my roll / I need a little steam heat on my floor."[20] "To an Admirer" expresses another common theme in women's blues: the speaker, having been hurt, distrusts her new man. Conversely, in "Confession," the speaker is both candid and bold as she rationalizes the freedom to express her sexuality without conventional constraints. She rejects, for instance, marriage and the traditional white wedding dress—which she describes tellingly as "that weary gown." The poem concludes,

> So, I must confess there've been other loves—
> But not even to them have I been true.
> For all the while my heart's real love
> Was burning through to you!

Here the speaker frankly defends her faithlessness, not just to her current lover, but to past loves as well; the poem thus nods toward the sexual and emotional freedom expressed in the lyrics of Rainey, Smith, and Holt.

According to the criteria established in Angela Davis's groundbreaking text *Blues Legacies and Black Feminism,* Lucia herself fits the description of a blueswoman. Davis explains that "the representations of love and sexuality in women's blues often blatantly contradicted mainstream ideological assumptions regarding women and being in love. These lyrics also challenged the notion that women's 'place' was in the domestic sphere." According to Davis, women's blues often "satirically accentuate the contrast between the dominant cultural construction of marriage and the stance of economic independence black women were compelled to assume for their sheer survival."[21] In "All That I Ask" (1925), Lucia explicitly rejects the economic, transactional aspect of marriage: "Merchants sell much that you may buy—/ All this I know is true. / But just your love, which can't be bought, / Is all I ask of you." Nevertheless, the blueswomen, much like Lucia, always sing unapologetically about physical love. In "Brief Song," written when Lucia was employed at Tuskegee, she celebrates "A long, long stretch of open road—/ A car that cuts the wind in two; / A humming motor that sings you to sleep, / And you—you—you!"

Pitts's love poems thus depict independent women, untrammeled by conventional, gendered roles and transactional relationships. Her poems do not, however, emulate Millay's rather hardened and sarcastic tone or the bitter cynicism of Ma Rainey and Bessie Smith; rather, like the clever lyrics of Nora Holt, they are wry, witty, and gently humorous; ironically detached; warm but not cloying.

Eventually, the tone and topics of Pitts's poetry changed. Her employment with the State of Illinois and the federal government in Washington, DC, and later her service in the army during World War II, exposed her to national and international issues and concerns. Not surprisingly, they wrought some changes on her verse; her later poems focus more critically on social justice while still maintaining an ultimately optimistic racial outlook for America.

Although Pitts's poetry never received mainstream recognition, it was admired by her contemporaries. In 1935, the lawyer and gospel songwriter William Henry Huff acknowledged both her lyrical skill and her administrative work in Roosevelt's government as he implored: "God bless the lady we call Lou, / Who deals in deals that we call new / And writes those lovely lines of love / That almost take your breath."[22] In 1938, the journalist and poet Frank Marshall Davis observed, "Lucia Mae Pitts in her creations bears out our opinion that she consistently writes the best love poetry produced among our women."[23] Earlier, Pitts had either anticipated—or perhaps received—criticism that she focused too much on love poems. She immediately saw that inherent in such a critique is the fact that love is dismissed as a "feminine" preoccupation, as opposed to the weighty subjects of male poets. Her 1928 poem "Decision" responds to such criticism with awareness and self-deprecating humor:

> I shall not sing of love so much—
>   It's foolish—awfully so.
> The world will think I know no else
>   And rate me very low.
>
> I can sing of other things—
>   Indeed—I really can.
> I'm not so awfully wrapped up
>   In the genus they call man.

Teasingly, she promises to explore other subjects and themes, only to reverse herself in the final stanza:

> I guess I'll write of the Darwin theory
>   Or, perhaps, of politics—
> Just to change my line: but you know
>   Such scribbling never sticks.
>
> Oh, pshaw! There's no use fooling you—
>   After all, I shall not change.
> If I did, at this late date,
>   You'd merely call me strange.

A review of Pitts's oeuvre shows that she continued, with great success, to compose love poems throughout her career. Her unabashed interest in love poetry is frank and honest; it shows a level of self-confidence that would serve her well in the federal government, where she was often the only Black person in the room, and especially in the military, where she met multiple challenges with humor and resilience.

A major influence on the life of Lucia Mae Pitts was her peripatetic family, to whom she was exceptionally close. While it may appear pedantic to detail the family's trajectory from Alabama, Georgia, and Tennessee to Boston, Chicago, and Detroit, their travels encapsulate the Great Migration and demonstrate how geography functions as a mode of resistance to racism and Jim Crow. Geographic mobility thus becomes the agency through which the Pitts family, symbolic of thousands of other African American families, ensured their survival, education, and economic success. Lucia Mae was born on January 17, 1904, in Chattanooga, Tennessee, to Janie A. Harris Pitts, a homemaker from Alabama, and Jarrett Thomas Pitts, a barber from Georgia. Janie and her sister Katie had moved from Alabama to Rome, Georgia; they were both literate, which was itself an accomplishment for the time and place. In Rome they met and married their spouses: Janie wed Jarrett Pitts and Katie married Isaac Ernest; the couples then migrated together to Chattanooga.

The 1910 census shows six-year-old Lucia living at 318 ½ Spring Street in Chattanooga with her parents and her two brothers, Harrison, age thirteen, and Jarrett Jr. (called Ralph), age eleven. Lucia is the youngest of five children and the only surviving girl. (Her sixteen-year-old sister Clara had died in September 1904, eight months after Lucia's birth.) Also residing in the home are Lucia's Aunt Katie Ernest and her daughter Rozelle Ernest. The family rents the house, and all the inhabitants can read and write. Lucia's two oldest brothers, Royal (or Roy, born in 1886) and Edgar (1895), have left Chattanooga and live in Chicago; eventually Harrison and Jarrett will join them. Some years later, Janie and her daughter Lucia will also move to Chicago. Edgar will eventually leave Chicago and make his home in Detroit. Although the family established themselves in Chicago, Edgar presumably moved to Detroit at the invitation of his and Lucia's half-sister, Lucille. Lucille's husband Irving Langston worked as a machinist at Ford Motor Company. Lucia would always remain close to Lucille, whose story is further emblematic of African American geography and upward mobility, and the sisters would live together in New York at the height of the Harlem Renaissance.

Lucille was the oldest of the Pitts siblings; she was born in Rome, Georgia, to Jarrett Pitts and his first wife, Sarah Barrett, on October 27, 1883. Sarah's sister Elizabeth Barrett had previously migrated to Boston, and after Sarah's death, Elizabeth Barrett Long and her husband Alonzo brought baby Lucille to Boston and raised her as their own.[24] Alonzo G. Long was employed by the Boston Museum of Fine Arts; the family, cultured and educated, belonged to Boston's aspirational Black middle class. Lucille graduated from prestigious Girls' High School in 1901. In Boston's liberal, Abolitionist tradition, African American students were welcomed at the city's premier public exam institutions: Boston Latin (founded in 1635), Girls' High School, and Girls' Latin. The African American novelist and journalist Pauline Hopkins had attended Girls' High in 1871; Lucia's contemporaries, the poet Helene Johnson and the novelist Dorothy West, attended Girls' Latin.

After graduating from Boston Normal School, Lucille became a teacher in predominantly Irish and Italian Medford, a suburb of Boston. In a few years she moved to Ohio and became a librarian at Wilberforce University. On May 5, 1917, the *Xenia Daily Gazette* reported the marriage of Irving Y. Langston of Detroit, Michigan, to Lucille W. Pitts of Wilberforce, Ohio.[25] After residing in Detroit for some years, the couple eventually moved back east to New York City. The sisters were always close, and, given their common education and aspirations, Lucille would certainly have encouraged Lucia's poetry.

When World War I erupted, Lucia's brothers Roy and Edgar immediately enlisted. Edgar served in Europe, where he was decorated by the French and Belgium governments, while Roy remained stateside, primarily in Virginia. Certainly, their patriotism and military service made an impression on their little sister. Around 1915, just prior to the race riots in the infamous "Red Summer" of 1919, Lucia and her mother left Chattanooga and joined the four brothers in Chicago. It is unclear if Lucia's father had died, thus prompting the move from Chattanooga, or if her parents had separated. Historian Jill Watts contends that Jarrett Pitts was deceased, but he may also have returned to Georgia. In June 1918, Harrison registered for the draft and listed J. T. Pitts of Suwannee, Georgia, as his nearest relative. Since his brother Ralph (J. T. Pitts Jr.) was working in Chicago as a bellboy, their father must have been in Georgia. Moreover, the 1920 US census shows Jarrett T. Pitts, a sixty-year-old barber, residing in Floyd County, Georgia.

In Chicago, Lucia and her mother lived on the South Side, at 4811

Indiana Avenue. The 2,200-square-foot home would remain in the family through the 1950s, when Harrison and his wife lived there.[26] Despite the probability that her husband was alive, Janie Pitts listed herself as a widow in the 1920 census.[27] In the absence of a father, Lucia looked to her older brothers for a paternal connection, and they in turn were protective of their baby sister. Roy, perhaps because he was eighteen years older, assumed the paternal role, and Lucia would periodically live with him and his wife, Frankie. In fact, when Lucia, at the age of thirty-nine, joined the WAC, she had to sneak out of Frankie and Roy's home. "On a cold winter's morning in December of 1943," she recalls, "I slipped out of the house in Chicago and finally offered myself to the Army of the U.S. Even then I was still going against the wishes of . . . my oldest brother Roy (that was why I had to slip out of the house). . . . Roy never told me exactly why, but I suspect he had heard and believed the scurrilous rumors that the WACs . . . were only in the Army for the 'entertainment' of the soldiers, and he was therefore dead set against my becoming one of them."[28] As World War I veterans, Edgar and Roy apparently objected to Lucia's joining an organization whose members they had seen using women for "entertainment."[29]

The Pitts brothers were not alone in their objections: Brenda Moore quotes Elsie Oliver, a Boston hairdresser and one of Lucia's battalion members, who also had to enlist secretly because "my parents would have never agreed for me to [join] the Army [so] I didn't say anything to them about it until I was in."[30] Although Pitts never encountered disrespectful treatment, the families' fears were not unfounded. Shortly after the 6888th deployed to Europe, Pitts's commanding officer "[Major] Charity Adams found out [about] a rumor . . . that the black women in our battalion were being used to accommodate the black male soldiers and she had a fit."[31] Major Adams quickly dispelled the scurrilous rumor.

Recreating the close bond they enjoyed in Chattanooga, the four brothers settled their families within a few blocks of each other in Bronzeville. Education and religion were important family values. The brothers all attended elite St. Edmund's Episcopal Church. Still extant, St. Edmund's is "one of the oldest and most renowned and active predominantly Black Episcopalian congregations in Chicago."[32] Janie saw to it that Roy, Ralph, and Lucia all graduated from high school, while Harrison and Edgar each completed four years of college. Edgar, the intellectual of the family, studied at Tuskegee Institute, Fisk University, and the Chicago School of Decorating.[33] In the early twentieth century, Edgar's education was a major accomplishment—as late as 1940, only one percent of African Americans held college degrees. Another family member, Lucia's second cousin, Charles Wilson Boyd, and his wife, Alva Maxey of Atlanta, lived near the Pitts family at 2801 South Prairie Avenue. Boyd's mother, Rozelle Ernest, and her own mother had lived with Lucia and her mother Janie Pitts in Chattanooga in 1910. After Janie and Lucia moved to Chicago, Rozelle had moved to Cleveland, where she married and started a family.

The Pitts brothers easily found work in Chicago; jobs were plentiful in the stockyards, steel mills, railroads, foundries, and in the hospitality sector. Having established themselves financially, the brothers married and purchased homes. Roy married Frankie J. Muirhead of Nashville, Tennessee, on Christmas Eve 1938, in Chicago.[34] He worked in hotels as a waiter, while Frankie held the unique position of lighthouse keeper, probably operating and maintaining lighthouses on Lake Michigan. After his first marriage failed, Edgar joined his sister Lucille in Detroit, where he worked as an interior decorator. In June 1938, he married Leora Powell, a college-educated secretary from Ohio.[35] The couple shared an interest in Black fraternal organizations; Leora was a member of the nation's oldest African American sorority, Alpha Kappa Alpha, while Edgar served as president of the Detroit chapter of Phi Beta Sigma fraternity.

Edgar and Leora's social life was avidly reported in the African American press. In March 1945, the couple hosted his sister, Lucille Pitts Langston, who was visiting from New York City. "A former Detroiter," noted the society columnist in *The Detroit Times*, "Mrs. Langston has been the recipient of many social courtesies extended by old friends." Edgar's brothers also visited Detroit: the society pages reported that "Mr. and Mrs. Roy Pitts and Mr. and Mrs. Harrison Pitts, of Chicago, were guests of their brother and sister, Mr. and Mrs. Edgar Pitts, of Chandler Avenue." While in the city, the brothers "rounded up many old friends."[36] Along with hosting his family, Edgar was deeply involved in the community—he was a supervisor of the State Emergency Relief Administration (SERA), president of the Joe Louis Boosters' Club, a member of both the American Legion and the Elks, and grand marshal in April 1942 of a March for Democracy parade. Edgar's commitment to racial progress and uplift would soon be emulated by Lucia.[37]

Lucia was particularly close to her brother Harrison. The two shared a love of music and poetry, and Harrison, a songwriter, introduced Lucia to contemporary rhythm and blues. After working on Beale Street in Memphis for W. C. Handy, Harrison became an accountant and co-owned several Bronzeville night spots with Edgar and Ralph. Located at 814 East 39th Street, Pitts Pub featured "fine beers, liquor, and wines" along with "Chinese and American dishes"; it was reported to be a "unique and intimate nitery" and "a favorite with after-dark fun seekers."[38] The venue's vibrant music scene was a big draw. A February 1946 *Chicago Bee* article reported that the glamorous rhythm and blues singer "Lil Palmore of Pitts Pub brought the house down with her songs, accompanying herself at the piano." Throughout the 1940s, Harrison penned several songs for Palmore, who was known in Chicago as "the Queen of the Blues," including "I Wanna Go Home" and "This Man of Mine."[39] Certainly, Harrison and Lucia discussed their mutual interests in writing poetry and the blues.

In July 1927, Harrison married Lucille Jones of Indiana.[40] In contrast to his brothers, who divorced and remarried, and Lucia, who never married, Harrison and Lucille were married for nearly fifty years. Their social life revolved around St. Edmund's Episcopal Church; in May 1958, the society page reported the handsome couple enjoying "a benefit banquet [for] St. Edmund's Episcopal Church"; the banquet was set to a Hawaiian theme, and "through the magic stairway of S. S. Aloha more than 200 guests enjoyed the glamorous fete sponsored by the Women's Auxiliary."[41]

The youngest brother, Ralph (J. T. Pitts Jr.), worked with his brothers in the hospitality business.[42] On July 23, 1919, Ralph and his wife Clarice Reed Pitts welcomed their son, and apparently Lucia's favorite nephew, Thomas LaVerne Pitts. Years later, during World War II, Aunt Lucia would dedicate a poem to her nephew, US Army First Lt. Thomas L. Pitts.

Educated at Chicago's Central YMCA College, the University of Illinois, and Northwestern University, Thomas Pitts pledged Kappa Alpha Psi fraternity. After basic training at Santa Ana Army Air Base in California, he was commissioned a second lieutenant. After the war, Captain Pitts returned home to Chicago, where he worked as an accountant with his Uncle Harrison and later opened his own business, Pitts Realty Company, on 79th and South Park Avenue. In March 1946, he married his college sweetheart, Lois Searcy, a social worker originally from Memphis, Tennessee.[43] "One of the most impressive weddings of the season," boasted a society reporter, "united lovely Lois Searcy and Thomas Pitts last Saturday at St. Edmunds Episcopal church."[44] Lois was a graduate of Central YMCA College and the University of Chicago and was a member of Alpha Kappa Alpha sorority. Their son, Dr. Thomas L. Pitts Jr., is a Northwestern University Medical School–trained physician who currently practices in Chicago.

Like her brothers and their offspring, Lucia also found success in Chicago. In fact, by the 1940s the Pitts family, only two generations removed from the depredations of bondage, were college-educated homeowners, comfortably ensconced in the city's African American professional class. Economic success did not, however, preclude service to the church and the community; racial uplift was a family value. Although the Pitts brothers had all joined elite St. Edmund's Episcopal, Lucia and her mother chose the equally renowned Pilgrim Baptist Temple. The pioneering pilot Bessie Coleman was a member of Pilgrim Baptist, and Dr. Martin Luther King Jr. would preach there during the 1960s civil rights movement. Part of the draw for Lucia was the church's music ministry: Aretha Franklin, Mahalia Jackson, Thomas A. Dorsey (who wrote "Take My Hand, Precious Lord"), and Rev. James Cleveland all sang at Pilgrim Baptist, which came to be known as the birthplace of gospel music. Lucia was active in the church; she and her friend Dorothea Pryor were the first youth directors. In 1922, Lucia drew on the church's talented membership and produced a musical pageant; she invited Bronzeville youth with a lively announcement: "You Young People Who Find Nothing Interesting At Church, Come To The Musical Pageant At The Pilgrim Baptist Temple 33rd and Indiana Avenue Monday, Apr. 24, '22 8:15 P.M. And See If You Don't Change Your Minds."[45]

In taking a leadership role at Pilgrim Baptist, Lucia was emulating her mother, Janie Pitts. Described in the newspaper as a "well-known church and social worker," Janie Pitts was the quintessential "church lady"; as a lay leader in a large and prosperous congregation, Janie would have modeled for her daughter the planning, budgeting, and organizational skills that stood Lucia in good stead while she was employed with the federal government. Like so many women of her generation, Janie found in the church the scope for her intelligence and abilities that was denied to her in domestic service jobs. When Janie Harris Pitts died on December 18, 1926, at age 59, after "a lingering illness," her funeral was held at Pilgrim Baptist Temple, with Lucia's friend Lillian Fowler-Shaver providing special music.[46] Lucia was devastated, but she found relief, in part, by penning a moving dirge, "I Have Heard Songs":

> Once it was a happy song,
> For out of the womb of her who lies
> Under that resisting sod came I—
> Blood of hers, and of her own flesh.
> But the song ends
> In a note that flings itself
> Against Fate, and breaks—
> A note that falls in tears.

She published the poem in 1929, in memory of her mother.

While Lucia was attracted to the music ministry of Pilgrim Baptist, she was interested in secular as well as sacred music. As a teenager, she formed the Harmony Quartet with four friends: the pianist Clare Alexander and singers Val Jeanne Morrison, L. Dorothea Pryor, and Laura Baxter.[47] Music would remain a central force in her life and in her poetry; she was greatly influenced both by the gospel music she encountered at Pilgrim Baptist, and the blues performers she would have discussed with Harrison and witnessed in her brothers' pubs in Bronzeville.

Living in Chicago, with family in the music business, Lucia would have heard the gossip about the unconventional private lives of Ma Rainey and Bessie Smith. She certainly knew Rainey's wittily candid "Prove It on Me Blues," and would also have known that Rainey and Smith, although technically married to men, were romantic partners. In 1925, when the

Chicago police arrested Rainey for hosting a "lesbian party," Bessie Smith bailed her out of jail the next morning. Free and defiant, Rainey penned her famous anthem of female sexual autonomy and love:

> They say I do it, ain't nobody caught me
> Sure got to prove it on me;
> Went out last night with a crowd of my friends,
> They must've been women, 'cause I don't like no mens.

Where Rainey and Smith did little to conceal their love lives, Lucia was more subtle and discreet about the identity and details of her lovers. In her poems Pitts carefully elides details about the sex or circumstances of her lovers; she does not "name names."

In 1925, Pitts wrote a series of poems for the "Lights and Shadows" column of the *Chicago Defender*, all of which allude to a painful, unrequited, and abortive relationship. "To An Admirer" (1925) warns that "men have made of my heart / A stone." Similarly, in "Fallen Castles" (1925) she uses both religious imagery and the metaphor of the twenty-four-hour clock to express the end of a love affair: "But life is so cold, and dreams are so short—/ My beautiful day has long fled. / And here stand I, unclothed, uncertain; / But a crown of pain on my head." Other poems suggest secret and complicated circumstances: in "I Shall Come to Thee" (1925) she announces: "Whene'er, where'er thou callest, thy voice I know well. / And tho thou callest from the depths of hell—/ I shall come to thee." Although this is strong language for a member of Pilgrim Baptist Temple, the poem also includes a warning: the speaker's heart "is no small thing with which to toy." The compressed, elliptical language of poetry thus enables Lucia to communicate intense but inexpressible feelings. If her poems were written to women or to married, gay, socially unacceptable, or otherwise unattainable men, it is quite possible that Lucia, given her family's position in Bronzeville society, may have needed to protect both her own privacy and that of her lovers.

Despite her early success on the local music scene, Lucia, perhaps guided by her brothers who knew the exigencies of the music and entertainment business, took a more pragmatic career path. Her brothers urged her to attend college after graduating from New Trier High School, but Lucia chose a business school, largely to gain employment quickly and help her mother financially. She recalled that "my mother and I searched for a good business school in Chicago" and selected an "an all-Negro school on Chicago's South Side."[48]

Lucia Pitts's decision to attend Chicago Commercial Institute was a propitious one and launched her professional career. After graduation, she was immediately hired by the prominent African American attorneys George C. Adams and Jesse N. Baker. Adams and Baker had founded the National Bar Association in August 1924 after Black lawyers were denied membership in the American Bar Association.[49] Much of their work involved civil rights cases, and Pitts's experience as a legal secretary would serve her well in subsequent jobs with the federal government. In September 1927, as a testament to her skills and abilities, she was recruited to Tuskegee, Alabama, where she worked as secretary for Dr. Eugene H. Dibble Jr., the medical director at Tuskegee Institute's John A. Andrew Memorial Hospital.[50] Dr. Dibble, a Howard University Medical School graduate, had completed his surgical residency at Andrew Memorial Hospital in 1923 and was named medical director in 1925. Along with her responsibilities at the hospital, where she claimed she had to "work like a Trojan," Pitts played an active role in the lives of the students; she organized and served as founding president of a Tuskegee chapter of the Chicago-based Diana Athletic Club, a prominent women's organization.

Shortly after arriving at Tuskegee, Lucia, who apparently had an "understanding" with another man in Chicago, met the handsome and talented Horace Mann Bond. Bond, then serving a one-year stint as director of the extension program at the State Normal School in Montgomery, was, like Lucia, born in Tennessee to ambitious, upwardly mobile parents. Pitts's poem "Brief Song" (1927) tantalizingly suggests a clandestine encounter they shared while driving along rural Alabama roads. To Lucia's chagrin, however, their connection was exposed in the pages of the *Chicago Defender*. After her Chicago swain learned of her friendship with Bond, he wrote a snide letter to Dewey Roscoe Jones, the editor of the

"Lights and Shadows" column, using Lucia's pseudonym The Lady Called Lou (TLCL). Jones then published the gossipy exchange:

> Dear Dewey R.: Pardon me, but it seems darn near time for some one to do some unbosoming. I find that I am accused of living in Montgomery—too close to Horace Mann Bond, but not close enough to Lucia. . . . But space and time are finite. So I'll bite—what IS the lowdown on HMB and Lucia?[51]

With an eye to generating interest in his column and thereby increasing its readership, Jones responded:

> And now it's out: Horace Mann Bond . . . fell in love with The Lady Called Lou, who, unfortunately for HMB, had already bestowed her affections on Hatch. They met in Montgomery, TLCL and HMB, and remembering H and H only, TLCL addressed HMB as H. Result, HMB is disillusioned. H . . . is befuddled and TLCL is repentant.[52]

In the paper's next issue, an astonished Lucia responded. Given how carefully she guarded her private life in her poems, she was understandably irate. She addressed her admirers in peremptory capital letters:

> I SAY—
> I'm going to sue somebody (and I strongly suspect it's Dewey R.) for spoiling my chances for matrimony. The man publishes to the world that I am in love with some one person—and that will never do—with all due respect to the person.
> Also, I'm going to sue HMB for being accessory.
> Let this end all this promiscuous slander.[53]

The three men, apparently not willing to tempt fate, ended their banter. Whether or not romance was actually involved, Lucia and Horace formed a lifelong friendship; Bond would eventually marry and become the father of civil rights activist Julian Bond.

Some years later, on a more serious note, Pitts wrote to Bond when he was a professor at Fisk University. She had written a series of sonnets, and she asked for his help securing a publisher for the volume, tentatively titled *Urns of Fate*. After noting that Countee Cullen had said "some grand things" about the manuscript, she added, "Lest you think a book of worth needs no pull with a publisher, I'd better explain these two points: publishers are shy about publishing *first books;* publishers are especially shy about publishing *first books of poetry*."[54] While Bond undoubtedly tried to help her, nothing came of the prospective volume. Thirty years later, Pitts penned a memoir on her groundbreaking experiences in the federal government entitled *The Little Fire and How It Grew*. Unfortunately, the publishing world was no more interested in the Black female experience in the 1960s than they had been in the 1930s.

After a year at Tuskegee, Lucia—homesick and "dream[ing] of the streets / of Chicago, the skyscrapers brushing lips / against the clouds, the lake the hustle and bustle"—resigned from her position at Andrew Memorial.[55] In July 1928, she was back home, working as a secretary for I. Jay Faggen, the manager of Bronzeville's legendary Regal Theater. Her new friend Corienne Robinson Johnson, a twenty-five-year-old newlywed, worked as Faggen's stenographer.[56] Lucia never forgot talented friends, and the two would reconnect years later in Washington, DC. The Regal was an exciting place to work; now demolished, it was a film, nightclub, and music venue and the inspiration for Harlem's Savoy Ballroom. The elegantly appointed theater boasted seating for three thousand people; although it was white-owned, it employed African Americans as staff and management.

In Chicago Lucia—vivacious, entrepreneurial, pretty, and popular—enjoyed a busy social life.[57] Her circle included Dewey Jones (now forgiven for his intrusion into her romantic life) and David Kellum at the *Chicago Defender;* Frank Marshall Davis, a poet and journalist at the Garvey-esque newspaper the *Chicago Whip;* Corienne Robinson Johnson at the Regal Theater; Lillian Fowler and Dorothea Pryor from Pilgrim Baptist; and Cecilia Goldsby, a poet and future army buddy with whom Lucia would serve in Arizona and in Europe as part of the 6888th Battalion. Years later, commenting on dating in the military, Goldsby would recall the lively social life she and Lucia had enjoyed in Chicago, even though "the competition there was keener" than on military bases. Goldsby advised her army sisters how to attract male soldiers: "It is well known that men like to talk about themselves. Encourage them to do so. Oh, yes, they will tell you some very unlikely tales. But, before they have completed one lie, ask a leading question that calls for a bigger lie. Keep 'em talking . . . Time to go now, see you later . . . No romance involved. BUT, there IS romance to be had."[58]

Lucia quickly reestablished her connection with the "Lights and Shadows" column in the *Chicago Defender*. When Dewey Jones, the column's editor, left for New York to pursue a master's degree in journalism at Columbia University, Lucia took over. Judging from the reviews, her term was largely successful. One reader wrote,

> Dear Lady Lou:
> We wish to congratulate you on the splendid work you are doing on the LAS column. It is well done and those that know us know that we are not given to flattery. We like your style, your sub-heads, your ready wit and breezy articles. . . . The column will grow greater with such a personality and we wish you success.[59]

While Pitts appreciated the compliment, she continued holding herself and her contributors to the highest standards. In an astute self-assessment, she apologizes for rejections but encourages her contributors to continue working: "Sorry, you whose contributions have not been quite up to scratch. Try again—write again—but we're going to make it hard for you to get in LAS—this is going to be a worthwhile column if we have to break our neck to get it done!"[60] As an editor, Pitts demanded quality work but was never prickly or pedantic, traits which served her well in future careers in government and the military.

Given her editor status, her sociable disposition, and her organizational and administrative skills, it is not surprising that Pitts would propose an annual conference of the LASers. She envisioned an event where LASers from across the country could meet, exchange ideas, and enjoy fellowship: "Wouldn't a get-together party be a nice thing for all the

Lasers—a sort of convention.... It could be held in Chicago.... I think it would promise so much enjoyment that several out-of-town Lasers would make the trip: and then, if it was quite successful, it could be an annual affair held in different cities."⁶¹ Although we do not know if the convention materialized, the proposal provides a window into Pitts's creative ingenuity, her outgoing personality, and her sense of fun.

One of Lucia's most intriguing encounters in Chicago was with Santie Sabalala, the urbane, British-educated Zulu poet and adventurer. Born in 1895 in a Kaffir tribe, he was "confirmed" by a witch doctor and "fangmarked" on his cheeks with ritual scarifications by his father. His mother, through missionary connections, sent him to England to escape the Boer War. There he learned to speak faultless English and sang in the internationally acclaimed Kaffir Boys Choir. Later he trained as an engineer, immigrated to Chicago, and wrote swashbuckling stories for *Adventure* and similar men's pulp magazines.⁶² Sabalala and Lucia moved in the same literary circles, and she would certainly have been impressed that Harriet Monroe published his work. A mutual friend was the journalist and poet Frank Marshall Davis. In his memoir *Livin' the Blues,* Davis recalls that "after meeting Lucia Mae Pitts, an attractive young poet, [Santie] asked me to arrange a marriage.... In return Miss Pitts, who was then working at the Regal Theatre, would have full use of his 'Rolls Royce town car with chauffeur.'" Davis adds, perhaps tongue-in-cheek, that the deal never came to fruition because, among other things, Santie "couldn't find his Rolls Royce."⁶³

Despite Davis's jocular tone, Santie and Lucia apparently developed a close relationship; his exotic, adventurous life would have appealed to her, along with shared interests in music, poetry, and travel. He may have been the subject of the poems she wrote between October 1928 and March 1929, which were at first passionate and exuberant and then heartbroken and crushed. Although she was characteristically mysterious about her lover's identity, the poem "Daring Me to Forget" (January 1929) offers a clue: "Where you have crucified me / Time and time again / There are scars—/ Scars that in the black of night / I touch tenderly—/ Because you made them." The image of scarring appears again in "I'll Sing My Songs" (March 1929), when the speaker says, "But my heart feels no want of tears—/ Of stinging pain that wounds and scars." One wonders if the references to scarring might allude to the ritual "fang scarification" on Santie's face.

In addition to a failed love affair, 1929 was difficult for Lucia in another way: her beloved mother Janie Harris had recently passed away. Lucia commemorated her in several poems, including the poignant "I Have Heard Songs." The lines celebrate Janie's life of hard work and indomitable courage: "Out there she lies, where nerveless hands / Thrust her tired body when at last / She came to road's end."

Although the 1929 poems are mournful, an optimistic note still prevails, and the existence of a new lover is implied in "Pagan": "'I go to bed singing / And I wake up singing,' / He said." In fact, Lucia's life seems to have been filled with music, family, and friends. Given the interest she and Harrison shared in music, they would certainly have enjoyed evenings at the Savoy Ballroom, a large, stylish dance hall near the Regal Theater where Lucia worked. The Regal and the Savoy were in the same block on South Parkway (now Martin Luther King Drive). The Sunset Café was nearby, on 35th Street, and the lively area was dubbed "the Harlem of Chicago." Among the performers at these venues, many of whom Pitts would have seen, were Count Basie, W. C. Handy, Billie Holiday, Lena Horne, Duke Ellington, Louis Armstrong, Fletcher Henderson, Ella Fitzgerald, Earl "Fatha" Hines, Aretha Franklin, and Bronzeville native Nat King Cole. Sadly, however, the impending Great Depression would soon have a devastating effect not only on the entertainment venues of Bronzeville but also on Lucia's economic situation. By 1930, many businesses in Bronzeville had closed, and Lucia lost the position at the Regal Theater. She recalls that "job openings being practically non-existent, and with more and more offices letting their help go, a couple of friends and I decided [to open] a public stenographic office."[64] The business did well at first, but "as the depression got worse, our situation began to worsen, until finally the days without any work at all were endless."[65]

As the depression worsened, government jobs became highly prized, and competition would have been intense, particularly for an African American woman. At this point, however, Lucia's fortunes improved. She was already a published poet and a popular local entertainer when the national Black press lauded her employment with the Illinois House of Representatives. In May 1931, *The Negro World*, the Harlem publication of Marcus and Amy Jacques Garvey's Universal Negro Improvement Association, announced that "Miss Lucia Mae Pitts, well known Chicago girl [*sic*], who has been employed at the state capitol in Springfield, Ill., for the past several months as a stenographer, has received high praise from the officials there, both colored and white." The paper added that "Miss Pitts has the further distinction of being the only colored girl employed in that capacity.... In addition to her business career Miss Pitts is perhaps better known as a poet of much ability."[66] Subsequent articles soon appeared in magazines and newspapers across the country. For example, *The Pittsburgh Courier* boasted that "the only colored of 20 stenographers in the House of Representatives," Miss Pitts "was said to be the best there."[67]

Despite her relief at finding work and the attendant glowing publicity, Lucia soon discovered to her chagrin that in Springfield Jim Crow was alive and well. Attempting to eat lunch, she discovered that "in this capital of the great state of Illinois and home of Lincoln, no restaurant would serve me."[68] Arriving at work, she noted, with wry understatement: "I was the only Negro in the stenographic pool.... The atmosphere... was cool, to say the least. Most of the other girls were from downstate Illinois and... downstate Illinois is closely akin to Mississippi."[69] Despite this inauspicious beginning, Lucia's charm, effervescent personality, work ethic, and technical skills disarmed her colleagues: "Gradually things warmed up in the stenographic pool... and the other girls began to thaw. One... told me quite frankly later that... she had never known an 'educated' Negro."[70] Before the end of the legislative session "we all became very chummy and they would sometimes bring me a hot lunch" from the segregated restaurants.[71]

Lucia always had a talent for being in the right place at the right time and meeting the right people. One day she met Mrs. Anna Wilmarth Ickes, the state representative from Winnetka and the wife of Harold L. Ickes, soon to be the US secretary of the interior. Anna Ickes, "a tall, stately white lady, walked in, looked the girls over and... walked over to me. She dictated some letters and asked if I could do all of her work thereafter."[72] Although this exclusivity was technically not allowed, a word to the Speaker of the House solved the problem. The two may have bonded over their shared North Shore background; New Trier High School was in Ickes's district, and she would have known of Lucia's superior education. However, Lucia always felt that Ickes chose her because she was naturally sympathetic to "the underdog"; Ickes was widely known for her advocacy for Native Americans, particularly the Navajo of New Mexico, and Lucia herself would eventually "observe first-hand the condition of the 'Race of Sorrows.'"[73] In any case, the meeting with Ickes would soon prove a propitious one.

After reactionary Springfield, Lucia was relieved to return to Chicago, but she was still out of work. Through brother Edgar's theatrical connections, she became a secretary to the actor Richard B. Harrison, best known for his portrayal of "De Lawd" in Marc Connelly's play *The Green Pastures*. Harrison was beloved in theatrical circles: during his five years and 1,657 performances in *The Green Pastures*, he became more reverent, gentle, and generous, as "his own personality seemed to fuse with that of the role he was playing."[74] Harrison seems to have taken a kindly interest in Lucia, and after the play's Chicago run ended, he suggested she join him in New York; he helped her to find work with the Federal Council of Churches. Another appeal of New York for Lucia was the opportunity to reunite with her sister, Lucille. In fact, the two lived together on Sugar Hill at one of Harlem's most exclusive addresses, 723 St. Nicholas Avenue. Named for the "sweet" life residents enjoyed there during the 1920s, Sugar Hill remains a picturesque neighborhood in West Harlem. Hurrying to work in the mornings, Lucia may have encountered fellow residents W. E. B. Du Bois, Duke Ellington, and future Supreme Court Justice Thurgood Marshall.

In New York, Lucia had her first experience with the *soi-disant* Harlem Renaissance. In addition to her church job, Pitts was employed by the flamboyant novelist and playwright Wallace Thurman.[75] Thurman's play *Harlem* had opened on Broadway, and Lucia may have met him through Richard Harrison. Dorothy West, a member of Thurman's avant-garde literary circle, described him as a slight man, "nearly Black . . . with the most agreeable smile in Harlem and a rich, infectious laugh" and a "deep and resonant" voice.[76] When Thurman suddenly decided to open a new magazine, he rented "an office on Seventh Avenue," installed a telephone, "and called in several young writers ... to help with the business of running the magazine."[77] Lucia, with her administrative skills, may have been one of the young writers; in fact, West herself may have worked for Thurman, in which case the two women would surely have met. Lucia probably also met the other members of Thurman's circle, including Countee Cullen, Langston Hughes, Zora Neale Huston, Bruce Nugent, and Eric Walrond.[78]

Lucia seems to have been unimpressed with the decadent and iconoclastic Harlem literati and probably felt that she could hold her own with any of them; she already had a substantial collection of poems that she showed to Countee Cullen. Cullen praised her work but did nothing to help her publish. She may also have discussed her poetry with Langston Hughes and Dorothy West; the latter published two of Lucia's poems in her literary magazine *Challenge* a few years later. In any case, Lucia did not stay long in New York: within ten months, thanks to her friendship with Anna Ickes, she obtained a sought-after federal position with the US Department of the Interior and moved to Washington, DC. A year later, in December 1934, Thurman died in New York City of complications from tuberculosis.

On September 5, 1933, Pitts became the secretary to Dr. Clark Foreman, a progressive Georgian, a member of Franklin Roosevelt's administration, and a special advisor on the economic status of Negroes to Secretary of the Interior Harold Ickes.[79] Once again, Lucia was a "first": Foreman would later chuckle that "when I gave the job to Lucia Pitts she was the first black secretary in government. Gene Talmadge, who was then the governor of Georgia, went on the radio twice a day and denounced me for doing such an outrageous thing."[80]

In addition to her government job, Lucia maintained her interest in poetry. She soon made friends with a circle of like-minded individuals including African American bibliographer and poet Beatrice Murphy, poet and journalist Tomi C. Tinsley, and Howard University graduate and poet John Burton. Murphy had graduated from prestigious Dunbar High School in Washington; like Lucia, she did not have the resources to attend college, so she opted for administrative work. As a secretary at Catholic University, she pursued her interest in collecting and cataloguing African American literature. Her dream was to anthologize the talented but unknown African American poets who published, as did she and Lucia, in the Black press.

Since Countee Cullen's volume *Caroling Dusk* appeared in 1927, no collections of African American poetry had been published. In addition, according to Murphy, "all previous anthologies of Negro poetry have been curiously alike. We knew exactly what names would be found inside the covers."[81] Here Murphy addressed what was surely a sore spot for Lucia: She had published extensively, had completed two poetry manuscripts, and had networked with prominent individuals like Countee Cullen, Langston Hughes, and Horace Bond, but she was still unable to break into the cadre of anthologized Black writers that included Cullen, Hughes, Arna Bontemps, Sterling Brown, Claude McKay, and others. In envisioning her anthology, Murphy maintained that "within the Negro race is a great deal of undiscovered talent and . . . it [is] the duty of any member of our race in a position to do so, to help bring this talent to light."[82] Lucia, having edited "Lights and Shadows" in the *Chicago Defender*, knew exactly how to help Murphy achieve her goals.

In the mid-1930s, Pitts and Murphy, along with John Burton, a teacher and graduate student at American University, formed an editorial board and found a publisher for their anthology, which they dedicated to the memory of James Weldon Johnson, himself a pioneer in Black literature and bibliography. They combed the Black press for poems, corresponded with authors, and secured permissions. Lucia, with her experience in formatting government publications, provided "cheerful and generous assistance with the mechanical composition of the book."[83]

In 1938, *Negro Voices* appeared to critical praise. The volume included a few "favorites" like Langston Hughes and Anita Scott Coleman, but the bulk of the book consisted of "eighty-three colored writers," including talented but unknown poets like Edythe Mae Gordon, as well as John Burton, Beatrice Murphy, and Lucia Pitts.[84] Lucia's old friend from Chicago, Frank Marshall Davis, wrote a glowing review of the book in the Kansas City *Call*, in which he promised that the volume would "revive general interest in Negro letters, prove to the skeptics that our bards are doing work comparable to that of whites, provide the race-conscious with a book they should be proud to own, and furnish poetry lovers" with an outstanding collection.[85] Davis also singled Pitts's love poetry out for special praise: Her love poems include "Requiem," "This Is My Vow," "Promise," and "Moment in Paradise." It must have been greatly rewarding to see her work at last in print between the covers of a book.

In many of Pitts's love poems the optimism of nature, especially in flowers and trees, is a recurring trope and one with which she testifies to the strength and resilience of the race. Like her contemporaries Helene Johnson and Anita Scott Coleman, Pitts draws on tree imagery in her love poetry, where it becomes an unabashed celebration of the sensuality of Black men. For example, Scott Coleman's poem "Portraiture" depicts African American men as "the tall trees that remain / Standing in a forest after a fire. / . . . For their roots are thrust deep / In the heart of the earth." Johnson mirrors this theme in the sultry lyrics of "Trees at Night," through which the reader experiences "Printed 'gainst the sky—/ The trembling beauty / Of an urgent pine." In the same vein, Pitts's "Forest at Dusk" captures "Tall, slender pines / Standing straight / Against a dusky sky." In describing the pines "Against the deepening darkness, / Clinging close together / As they climb / Toward Heaven," Pitts suggests the challenges endured by the race, as well as the uplift for which she worked so tirelessly throughout her life. However, the poem's sensual descriptions of the "drowsy bird / In the shadows" and the "tingling, piney odor" make it clear that this is also a love poem. In fact, one of Pitts's special talents was the ability to broaden the scope of her love poetry to encompass her passionate commitment to her country and to her race.

The dramatic and striking description of pines "Clinging close together / As they climb / Toward Heaven" also points to a religious core undergirding much of her verse. Janie Pitts clearly instructed her children in moral behavior and self-control and taught them charity toward the less fortunate. These values are evident in Lucia's life, from her role as a church youth leader while a teenager to her decision to join the armed forces to her later work as a Red Cross volunteer in Washington, DC, and Los Angeles, and they are also manifest in her poetry.[86] For example, selflessness, love of country, and concern for the race lie at the heart of

"A WAC Speaks to a Soldier"; the poem's speaker personally sacrifices for her country and empathetically sees the perspective of male soldiers marching off to war: "We send you forth, / And as you go marching in never-ending files, / With our hearts and the work of our hands / We salute you." Similarly, "Letters" illuminates Pitts's recurring religious imagery and spiritual tone. She borrows from African American colloquialism when she writes:

> God, how they help—those little squares!
>   Letters from folk who care—
> They're blessings in disguise—salve for the soul—
>   And they make every day wondrous fair.

When she published "Letters" in 1928, Pitts could not have known that the poem would perfectly anticipate her service, two decades later, with the 6888th Central Postal Directory Battalion, as well as the battalion's motto, "No Mail, No Morale." In terms of critical tools, then, much of Pitts's deftly drawn verse invites readings through the lens of theology and philosophy as well as literature and music.

Despite the demands of her government job, the pressure of always being a "first," and the editing of *Negro Voices,* Lucia found time to organize and direct a music hour concert series, to write more poems, and to keep in touch with her Chicago friends.[87] Writing to Dewey Jones in February 1934, she entreated,

> Let lasers know, near and far,
> I still occasionally twang my guitar
> But am so involved in the nation's work
> It seems as if I have to shirk
> The poetic muse and L. A. S.
> For all this heavy business.

In a postscript she added happily: "To be more explicit, I have that rare thing—a job—as secretary to Dr. Clark Foreman in the U.S. Department of the Interior."

Over the next few years, Pitts's poetic reputation expanded. In 1934, she published "The Kiss," one of her most sexually explicit and erotic poems, in Dorothy West's new, Boston-based literary journal *Challenge*. The following year, West published Lucia's "Challenge": "Love, I adore your timid tenderness / [. . .] You are so sweet—so sweet! I love you much. . . . / But I am raging flame. Dare you to touch. . . . !" Although the poem is characteristically oblique, the object of the poem seems to be a woman; one wonders whether Pitts is adopting a male speaker's persona or whether, in fact, she had become romantically involved with a woman in Washington, DC. She was also invited to contribute poems to *American States Anthology* (1936), a regional compendium of poetry edited by Gerta Aison for Galleon Press. Lucia's work with the federal government, however, occupied most of her time. On Easter Sunday 1939, Secretary Ickes famously invited Marian Anderson to perform at the Lincoln Memorial after the segregationist Daughters of the American Revolution (DAR) refused to allow her to sing in their DAR Hall. That February, the association of federal secretaries and stenographers, the FGSS, had selected Lucia as a delegate to the Marian Anderson Protest Committee.[88] Given her connections to Secretary Ickes, it seems safe to assume that Pitts played a role in informing him of Anderson's situation and in facilitating the Lincoln Memorial concert. In fact, Lucia would first have heard Anderson sing at her very own Pilgrim Baptist Church in the 1920s.[89]

Pitts would long have a warm spot for Secretary Ickes, for Mrs. Anna Ickes, and for President Roosevelt; she credited Mrs. Ickes with "changing the course of my life—all for the better,"[90] and she wrote a poignant elegy, "Franklin Delano Roosevelt," on the president's death in April 1945. In the poem, she celebrates the late president as a Moses figure, a great man who in leading the charge for a more inclusive America, "gave his life to the cause / For which Christ long ago gave His: / The cause of justice, and mercy, and peace."

While in DC, Lucia was heavily involved in the recruitment of other Black women into the civil service. She explained, "Knowing what it was to be a Negro girl trying to make her way with several odds against her from the beginning, I wanted very much to help others."[91] Her first recruit was an old friend from the Regal Theater in Chicago, Corienne

Kathleen Robinson. When Clark Foreman chose the Harvard-educated, African American economist Robert C. Weaver as his associate adviser, Lucia picked Corienne Robinson to be Weaver's secretary.[92]

A year younger than Lucia, Corienne was from rural Jacksonville, Illinois, just north of St. Louis. Her high school yearbook photo reveals a beautiful young woman with a bright smile. Next to her senior portrait is the inscription, "Blessed are those with a sense of humor," which suggests that the two women were likely kindred spirits. Reconnecting in November 1933 in Washington, they briefly shared a house on Columbia Road NW; after a winter meeting of coworkers, the group drove to their home "for refreshments and entertainment."[93] Corienne had divorced Johnson, her first husband, and would remarry in June 1950, this time to Yale University graduate and career army officer Maj. William Morrow.[94]

In 1938, Lucia Pitts and Dorothy Embry of the Works Progress Administration, Arabella Denniston and Harriet West of the National Youth Administration, and Corienne Robinson of the US Housing Authority cofounded an organization composed of women employed as federal secretaries and stenographers, the FGSS, later named the Outer Guard. Along with fostering recruitment, the group aimed to help new employees adjust to the routines and rigors of government employment.[95] As part of these efforts, Lucia Pitts published a lengthy self-improvement essay titled "Written for Women." Commissioned by the Chicago-based Associated Negro Press (ANP), which serviced over one hundred papers, the article offers advice on hygiene, dress, hair, make-up, efficiency, attitude, honesty, and resistance to unwanted sexual advances. The ANP editor noted that "with the great influx of girls coming to Washington to accept jobs, the Washington correspondent's interest was aroused when the Outer Guard held a meeting to try to assist and counsel these young women. As a result, Miss Lucia Pitts consented to do an article . . . for the good and welfare of all young women entering the business and professional world."[96] "Written for Women" is full of wisdom acquired from Pitts's long years of service in private and government offices; it reads precisely like what a mother might tell her daughter when she first starts to work.

Pitts authored another important essay, "The Negro Marches On," in

1935, apparently for delivery in the District's public schools. She begins with an apologia, justifying the essay's focus on race:

> I do not believe in too much race consciousness—especially that kind which keeps us a race apart instead of allowing us to feel that we are just a part of the great human race. But I do believe in that race consciousness which makes us fight together to achieve as a group. I believe we should be justly proud of those Negroes who have forged ahead and made great names for themselves in some line of endeavor.

Because we "know too little of these people," she highlights the accomplishments of eight contemporary African Americans in different fields: in painting, the Chicago painter and playwright Charles Sebree (1914–1985); in social work, the Chicago social worker and dean of women at Hampton Institute Faith Jefferson Jones (1905–1971); in law, the Chicago attorney and judge Edith Spurlock Sampson (1901–79); in acting, the dramatic reader and Broadway star Richard B. Harrison (1864–1935); in business, the Richmond, Virginia, bank president and civic leader Maggie L. Walker (1864–1934); in publishing, W. A. Scott (1902–1934), of the *Atlanta Daily World* and the Scott Newspaper Syndicate; in government, Dr. Robert C. Weaver (1907–1997) of the US Department of the Interior; and James Weldon Johnson (1871–1938), the lawyer, musician, United States Consul, secretary of the NAACP, professor, novelist, and poet.

Pitts's many essays have been ignored, but they constitute a significant part of her oeuvre. Along with helping us to know and appreciate her, they display a generosity of spirit and passion for bringing people together by emphasizing excellence. They range from "The Negro," a historical sketch used in military orientation classes; to an article in Rev. Adam Clayton Powell Jr.'s weekly Harlem newspaper urging the US employers to hire able Blacks; to a series on "The Back Streets of Business," commissioned by *The Pittsburgh Courier*.[97] Throughout the essays, Pitts expands on many of the tropes that recur in her poetry: humor, wit, wisdom, and a concern for the race. In fact, had she not found the federal government more fulfilling, she could easily have worked full time as a journalist.

Pitts continued to write poetry, and in 1940 she submitted her poem "Let Them Come to Us" to the American Negro Exposition. The exposition, also known as Chicago's Black World's Fair, celebrated the 75th anniversary of the emancipation of enslaved people in the United States. The fair spanned three months, from July to September, and included scores of exhibits: paintings, dioramas, murals, sculptures, and newspapers, as well as displays from businesses, governments, schools, fraternal organizations, women's clubs, and the country of Liberia. Live entertainment included performances by Duke Ellington, Paul Robeson, and dozens of others, while Langston Hughes and Arna Bontemps contributed a musical, "Jubilee: Cavalcade of the Negro." The poetry contest featured over three hundred poems from approximately two hundred poets. Melvin Tolson received the $50 first prize for "Dark Symphony"; Pitts won an honorable mention for "Let Them Come to Us," triumphing over her friend Gwendolyn Brooks.[98]

In June 1940, with conditions worsening in Europe as Hitler's troops marched into Paris, President Roosevelt ordered the creation of a National Defense Advisory Commission (NDAC). The commission's top priority, notes Walter B. Hill Jr., was "the equitable employment of all groups of Americans in the rapidly growing defense industries."[99] To that end, NDAC hired Dr. Robert Weaver as chief of its Negro Employment and Training Branch; Weaver in turn hired the distinguished journalist Ted Poston as his assistant, and he recruited Lucia Pitts away from the Department of the Interior. In July, Pitts joined the two men at NDAC and subsequently on the War Production Board. Years later, she recalled that

> when the Women's Army Auxiliary Corps came into being in May of 1942, I wanted to dash right out and be among the first to join up. But I was then working as an Administrative Assistant for Robert Weaver in one of the defense agencies of the federal government in Washington and, idiot that I was, I let him convince me that his office needed me more than the WAAC did.[100]

Pitts finally stepped down from her position in December 1942, after a decade in Washington; she returned home to Chicago, where she lived with her brother Roy at 5156 Michigan Avenue and worked as the first African American personnel director in the Chicago bureau of the US Department of the Treasury.

Coincidentally, the Chicago Urban League met with local US Treasury Department officials in December 1942. The department, "under heavy fire for its segregationist policies,"[101] eventually announced that it would stop discriminating against its Chicago-based African American employees, and it hired Lucia Pitts to handle "complaints arising from Negro employees of the Department."[102] At year's end, Pitts resigned from the Treasury Department; on Thursday morning, December 16, 1943, in one of her most rewarding and consequential decisions, she enlisted in the US Army's Women's Army Corp.[103]

With her friends arguing that she was too independent to take orders, and her protective older brothers insisting the army was no place for a lady, Pitts was determined to prove them wrong. For basic training, she reported to Fort Des Moines, Iowa, in January 1944. Fort Des Moines had been established as the army's first training site for women during World War II and provided extensive courses in map reading, physical fitness, teamwork, discipline, marching, first aid, and army regulations. At the end of training, a delighted Lucia became Private Pitts, and she received her first operational assignment—to Fort Huachuca, Arizona. Near the Mexican border and Tucson and nestled beneath mountains, Fort Huachuca was, according to Pitts, "the largest Negro military installation in the world."[104] The post newspaper, *The Apache Sentinel,* trumpeted her arrival in its April 7, 1944 issue, declaring "Talented Pvt. Lucia Pitts Welcome Addition to WAC." The article reviews her long list of accomplishments and underscores that "few women enjoying such a colorful and successful career have voluntarily put it aside to serve, where best they may, with the armed forces."[105]

Assigned to the office of the provost marshal, the officer in charge of the post's military police, Private Pitts understudied and eventually replaced the male sergeant major, but with the title acting sergeant major. In that capacity, she supervised the administrative clerks and was ultimately responsible for all the office work. As an inspector documented,

"Acting Sergeant Major Lucia M. Pitts has charge of all clerical work, which includes fingerprinting and records of whiskey and marihuana cases as well as the many minor infractions of the law."[106] A particular highlight was a visit to Fort Huachuca on March 25, 1944, by Langston Hughes, whom Lucia had probably met in New York. He sought her out and flattered her by autographing a copy of his poem "The Negro Mother."[107]

Meanwhile, Lucia continued to write and publish her poetry. She sent most of her poems back to her family in Chicago for safekeeping; however, she published two in the Fort Huachuca newspaper: "A WAC Speaks to a Soldier" and "From the Heart." "A WAC Speaks to a Soldier," the more radical of the two, is a long love letter to her African American brothers in arms. The poem's most poignant moment comes in stanza two, when the speaker confronts male attitudes on domesticity, submissiveness, and the woman's place:

> You did not really want us here.
> "Women have no place in the Army," you said.
> "Women should stay at home and keep the home-fires burning.
> We want to think of you as sitting and waiting
> For us to come back,
> Dressed in the flimsy gowns which were yours alone . . .

The WACs were not, however, the demure and tractable women that some anticipated. The speaker explains,

> We have swallowed your disapproval
> And joined up just the same,
> Because there was a job to be done
> And we had to do it.

In defying their partners' edicts, the women displayed their commitment to their country. Moreover, they claimed their space in a threatening and unpredictable American landscape.

Pitts's speaker was right to admire these intrepid young women, whose arrival in the army occurred only after the African American community vigorously protested the discrimination toward Black nurses by the Department of War. The brave Mabel Keaton Staupers, Executive Secretary of the National Association of Colored Graduate Nurses, infuriated by such blatant exclusion, led a successful campaign, supported by First Lady Eleanor Roosevelt, Mary McCloud Bethune, and Representative Adam Clayton Powell Jr., to admit Black women to the army. Pitts dedicated her poem to the soldiers at Fort Huachuca, to her nephew, Lt. Thomas L. Pitts, and "to all soldiers in order that they may better appreciate what the Women's Army Corps stands for."

A week later, on a lighter note, the WACs selected their annual "pin-up boy." For some time, the male soldiers had held "Sweetheart" contests, with photographs of charming female friends; they also routinely solicited pictures of their favorite stars, such as the gorgeous actress Lena Horne. Now, engaging in the fun and boosting their morale, the WACs designed their own contest. They eventually chose First Lt. Thomas L. Pitts, of the US Army's Quartermaster Corps in England, as their winner. The muscular young soldier's military photograph, with his silver lieutenant's bar and gold propeller and wings prominently displayed, is striking. Accompanying the photograph is the writeup, "WACs Pick Pin-Up." The article names Lieutenant Pitts the contest winner and announces that he is the son of Mr. and Mrs. Ralph Pitts of Chicago and the nephew of Private First-Class Lucia M. Pitts.[108]

The Pitts winning streak continued, as Lucia learned that she had passed the written examination for commission as an officer. But she decided to forego Officer Candidate School in order to accept an overseas assignment. After a brief trip to Chicago over the 1944 Christmas holidays, she reported to Fort Oglethorpe, Georgia, where she and five hundred other women were put through "intensive training, including a five-mile hike . . . under active war conditions."[109] During her leisure time, Pitts honed her musical skills as an active member of the choir. She recalls that a new "responsibility somehow got to be mine at Oglethorpe: I became director of our Company choir. . . . Though I had consorted a lot with musicians and once did some singing, I am not a musician. But the choir got many compliments and my assignment stuck throughout our stay in England."[110]

Pitts and her cohort, the 6888th Central Postal Directory Battalion, would soon become the first African American WACs to serve overseas in an active war zone. Toward the end of January 1945, the 6888th left Georgia for Camp Shanks, a major embarkation post near the Hudson River in New York. They departed for Europe on February 3, on board the SS *Île de France;* eight days later, after dodging German U-boats in the Atlantic, they arrived in Scotland. Pitts would serve on the continent, primarily in England and France, for the next six months before being discharged in August 1945 at the end of the war.

The 6888th, nicknamed the "Six Triple Eight" and commanded by Wilberforce University alumna Maj. Charity Adams, was the army's only all-Black, all-female battalion to serve overseas.[111] The unit was tasked with tackling a massive backlog of mail from loved ones back home and getting it to the roughly four million troops, government workers, and Red Cross volunteers in the European theater. Pitts offered the following firsthand account of her daily activities:

> The job of our battalion, the 6888th Central Postal Directory, was to keep up with the addresses of our fighting men, who were almost constantly on the move, and see that their mail reached them. Under the general command of Major Charity Adams . . . the WACs did a noteworthy job of cleaning out the . . . letters and packages we found piled up like mountains when we arrived, then keeping up with those constantly arriving. An average of 30,000 address changes had to be made every day. I worked as administrative NCO . . . and had to keep the records, so I know whereof I speak.[112]

Pitts's account is easily corroborated by several sources.

In recognition of the battalion's work, Fort Lee Army post in Virginia (originally named for the Confederate States general Robert E. Lee) was renamed Fort Gregg-Adams, after Lt. Gen. Arthur J. Gregg, the army's first African American lieutenant general, and Lieutenant Colonel Adams, the

6888th Postal Battalion commander. On November 30, 2018, the army honored the 6888th with a majestic monument at the Buffalo Soldier Monument Park at Fort Leavenworth, Kansas. And on March 14, 2022, President Biden signed a bill awarding the 6888th Central Postal Directory Battalion the nation's highest honor, the Congressional Gold Medal.

The heroics of the Six Triple Eight have even emerged in popular culture: the Grammy Award–winning actor Blair Underwood recently announced an upcoming Six Triple Eight musical. In addition to the musical, in 2024, filmmaker Tyler Perry's movie *The Six Triple Eight,* about Major Adams, Cpl. Lena Derriecott King, and the women of the 6888th Battalion, debuted on Netflix. Kerry Washington played Adams, and Ebony Obsidian, Moriah Brown, Oprah Winfrey, and Susan Sarandon appeared in supporting roles. The movie is based on the 2019 article published by historian Kevin Hymel in *WWII History* magazine. Hymel interviewed Corporal King, and her account, for the most part, tallies with Lucia Pitts's memoir. One disparity in the two accounts, however, involves the tragic death of three WACs in Rouen, France. King says the women were on military assignment, while Pitts recalls that they had gone on a social outing to one of the men's camps. Pitts reports that two of the women died instantly, while the third died in a hospital a few days later. Perry dramatizes the fact that the women were denied admission to a local hospital; Pitts refutes this with an account of a Jeep accident suffered by her nephew around the same time; he was admitted to the local hospital "for some time," and she visited him there and describes the care he received.[113] While these are small discrepancies, they are important additions to the historical record.

The 6888th served initially in Birmingham, England; then, after approximately three months, they moved to Rouen, France. Lucia would always remember her visits to London and nearby cities, which were like "walking in a dream to see so many of the places about which I had read and heard for so long." She was partial to Shakespeare's birthplace, Stratford-upon-Avon, and to Westminster Abbey, Big Ben, and the Tower of London. And, of course, she remembered "the Englishman who asked me to marry him and stay in England!"[114] In Rouen, she was elated to learn that her nephew, Lt. Thomas Pitts, was stationed nearby. But there were strict rules about fraternization between officers and enlisted personnel. "It was a novel experience," she recalled, "to have to get special permission to go out with my own nephew!"[115] She was so enamored with Paris, "that famed City of Lights," that she returned years later, after her retirement.

According to Brenda L. Moore, "an estimated 855 African American Wacs, 824 enlisted women and 31 officers, served with the 6888th [Battalion]."[116] The battalion consisted of five companies, each with roughly 170 individuals. Pitts was a member of the 6888th Battalion's Company B, commanded by First Lt. Vashti B. Tonkins, of Gloucester County, Virginia.[117] After graduating from Hampton Institute (now Hampton University), Tonkins moved to St. Helena Island, South Carolina, where she taught at the renowned Penn School, an institution committed to the preservation of the Gullah culture. She returned to Virginia in August 1942 and joined the Women's Army Auxiliary Corps, subsequently becoming one of the army's first Black women officers. On a fine summer day in Rouen in May 1945, in celebration of the victory by Allied forces in Europe, Lieutenant Tonkins led Company B in a majestic march at the marketplace where Joan of Arc had been executed. The photo of the WACs of Company B marching in their crisp uniforms shows the enormous pride felt by Pitts, Tonkins, and their sister soldiers in their contribution to the war effort.

Shortly after the war, Tonkins returned to civilian life and utilized the GI Bill to receive her master's degree in education from the University of Chicago; she then worked as a teacher and later an administrator in the Philadelphia, Pennsylvania, school system. Afterward, Tonkins and her husband, WWII veteran Elwood Willis, a tailor and childhood friend, returned home to Hayes, Virginia, where they retired. One of the last surviving members of the 6888th, Lieutenant Tonkins Willis died on June 7, 2000, at the age of ninety.[118]

Other members of Company B chose to remain in the military; several served in WWII, the Korean conflict, and the Vietnam War. Pitts noted, for example, "My friend Ruth Jacobs . . . retired in 1964 after 20 years' service; my friend Novella Auls retired in 1967 after 25 years." Of her WAC pals, Lucia was probably closest to Ruth Sarver Jacobs and Novella

Auls. Ruth Sarver (later Mrs. Marcellus Burnett Jacobs) was Lucia's Chicago neighbor, a graduate of the Chicago Music School, and a classically trained violinist. Coworkers at the War Department, they joined the WAC in 1944 and soon volunteered for overseas duty; whereas Lucia desired "to show [her] patriotism and satisfy the urge to travel," Ruth knew she would like the work since it was "very similar to that of [her] old government job with the War department."[119]

Lucia Pitts and her friend Novella Auls met at Fort Huachuca, Arizona, where they and eighteen others were barrack-mates. Novella worked at the post theater and Lucia with the military police.[120] Auls was from Cincinnati, Ohio; her parents and two older siblings moved from Alabama to Ohio just before her birth, and family considerations undoubtedly led her to attend Alabama State Teachers College in Montgomery, where she was a star athlete. After completing her studies, she joined the WAC in February 1943, from Montgomery.[121] While on active duty, she played on military softball, volleyball, and basketball teams, and she won prizes in track and field as a sprinter and high jumper. A March 1944 *Arizona Daily Star* article praised her basketball prowess: "A bevy of Ft. Huachuca Wacs returned to Ft. Huachuca yesterday after battling to a narrow 20–18 basketball victory over the USO Hostesses. . . . High scorer for the Wacs was Novella Auls with 12 points." That summer, Auls used her power-hitting and sure fielding at third base to lead the Fort Huachuca softball team to a WAC championship. In 1955, she competed successfully in the army's European WAC-WAF volleyball tournament in Munich, Germany.[122] Coincidentally, one of Lucia Pitts's duties at Fort Huachuca was to write plays that were "sung, danced and acted out by [her] sister WACs," including Novella Auls.

Not surprisingly, the athletic, multitalented Auls excelled as coach of the 6888th Battalion softball team. One of the players, Gertrude Cruse LaVigne, whom Pitts and Auls knew from Fort Huachuca, recalls that in August 1945 the team traveled to Namur, Belgium, to play in a tournament. Although they did not win the tournament, they enjoyed the remaining games. According to LaVigne, "While we were spectators in the bleachers for the remainder of the tournament, the two teams playing the championship started fighting on the field. A soldier stood up and shouted: 'Ladies, ladies, let's be gentlemen please.' This seemed to settle and quiet the teams, and they went on to finish the game." LaVigne confirms that "one officer, 1st Lt. Violet Hill, was among the players. Novella Auls was the team's coach."[123] In 1967, Auls retired from the army at the rank of staff sergeant and made her home in Newport News, Virginia.[124]

It was in Le Havre, France, in August 1945 that Pitts learned of Japan's surrender, ending World War II. Overjoyed, she "jumped up, screamed, [and] cried." Shortly afterwards, she boarded the *Thomas H. Barry* for the return journey to Staten Island, arriving on Monday, August 20, "amidst a loud and enthusiastic reception from the boats that came out to meet us." Reflecting on her army days two decades later, she testified to the intensity of her military experience: "The bond between WACs is strong, whether in touch or out of touch and I, for one, will remember and hold dear all of them. They became an indelible and important part of my life when we shared the great WAC adventure."[125]

After disembarking in New York, Lucia returned to Chicago; she received an honorable discharge from the US Army on August 24, 1945, from Brig. Gen. John T. Pierce, the commander of Fort Sheridan Army Post in Illinois. Her family was still in Bronzeville, but she chose to return to Washington, DC, to the Sherman Avenue neighborhood where she had lived in the 1930s. Situated one-half mile northwest of Howard University, the Sherman Avenue corridor was a predominantly Black area of apartment buildings, row houses, and mature trees—it would have reminded her of her happy days in Chicago. From Sherman Avenue, Pitts could access the entire city via public transportation; a brief bus ride would have brought her to the U Street District for shopping and entertainment, to her job at the US Capitol, or to her church, All Souls Unitarian, on Harvard Street NW.

Lucia had joined All Souls Unitarian after a long search for a church home. She had initially gone there for the funeral of former Secretary of the Interior Harold Ickes. Upon a return visit on Sunday, November 15, 1953, she found the service and the sermon enthralling; they were exactly what she had been looking for in a church, and she "joined up immediately." The pastor, Dr. Arthur Powell Davies, was a leading intellectual and prolific writer who championed civil rights. "Dr. Davies was not only a learned and deeply spiritual man, from whom I learned a great deal," she confessed, "but also, like Mr. Ickes, he was fearless in speaking out against racial injustices and in matching his deeds with his words."[126] Pitts would have also been attracted to the upscale, multiracial congregation. The church's Black members included mathematics teacher Norma Elizabeth Bond, a Howard University graduate and cofounder of Alpha Kappa Alpha sorority; World War II veteran Sharkey Boyd and his wife Julia; and attorney Bernice Just, whom Dr. Davies appointed director of religious education in 1957. Given her lifelong love of music, Pitts joined the church choir. Still extant, All Souls remains a progressive church, advocating for such causes as immigrant rights, voting rights, and marriage equality.

Though she would eventually return to the civil service, Pitts decided to try her hand in the private sector. In June 1946, the *Chicago Bee* reported that "if plans now being perfected work out, Washington will have a greatly needed personal service bureau. This bureau will take telephone calls in your absence from home and generally aid persons who are personally called away on business. Divided into a business and social division, the service sponsored by Lucia Pitts will soon be in operation."[127] Regrettably, the bureau was for the most part a disappointment. Although work requests came in, most of the jobs required typing, which aggravated Pitts's arthritis, brought on by so many years of working as a stenographer. She notes in *The Little Fire and How It Grew* that after two years, she closed the service bureau and found work as an assistant in a stationery shop.

In January 1949, Pitts returned to the federal government, this time with the Housing and Home Finance Agency (HHFA). She had recruited her friend Corienne Robinson in 1933; now Robinson, having attended night school at Howard University and graduated magna cum laude, returned the favor. Corienne was a racial relations officer and assistant in HHFA to Dr. Frank Horne, the ophthalmologist, poet, and former president of Fort Valley Normal and Industrial School (now Fort Valley State University). Horne, the agency's director of the Office of Race Relations, needed a secretary, and Robinson talked Pitts into taking the position.[128] She would remain with housing agencies until her retirement, rising into "the upper classification of government employees" as an intergroup relations officer.[129]

Although busy with her full-time job, Pitts found time for various volunteer activities. In addition to her participation at All Souls Unitarian, she volunteered with the Red Cross, primarily as a driver. She also felt a special bond with the WACs, and in 1947 she organized a meeting in Washington. As reported in the press, "Lucia M. Pitts . . . sent out questionnaires to a sampling of WAC veterans over the country, asking whether they would be interested in a WAC veteran gathering in Washington and possible organization." The organization would be open to "all women veterans of the United States . . . regardless of race, creed, color or national origin, and regardless of the branch of the service." For Lucia, having witnessed the transformative power of contact across the color line, it was important that the new organization embrace all WACs. She remembered, for instance, that as her unit was separating from service, "two of the white girls—one from Georgia, the other from Virginia—came to our rooms and said to us, 'It's been a pleasure knowing you girls. We have learned something and you have demanded our respect. We're proud of you.'" The news blurbs added that Pitts was supported in her efforts to organize the WACs by Capt. Dovey Johnson Roundtree, a former WAC (who would become a celebrated civil rights attorney), and by the educator and activist Dr. Mary McLeod Bethune, whom Pitts dubbed "Our Great Lady."[130]

Dr. Bethune had recruited Dovey Johnson for the first contingent of African American women officers in the WACs. After graduating from Spelman College in 1938, Johnson taught for three years at Finley High School in Chester, South Carolina. She then moved to Washington, DC, and worked for Bethune, who was both the president of the National Council of Negro Women (since 1935) and director of Negro Affairs at the National Youth Administration (since her appointment by President Roosevelt in 1936). Lucia Pitts met Dovey Johnson through Dr. Bethune's assistant, Arabella Denniston, a longtime government worker and co-founder, with Lucia, of the Outer Guard.[131] Following the war, Johnson studied at Howard University School of Law and married her college beau,

William Roundtree. "He was so tall and so handsome," she blushed years later, "that I'd taken note of him the first time that I saw him [at Morehouse College]."[132] Unfortunately, the marriage was short-lived, as Dovey immersed herself in her legal studies and William rejoined the army.

During her years in Washington, Lucia would have heard the term "the Secret City" used to describe "the web of streets and neighborhoods where 'colored folk' lived and worked and traded, cut off from whites as by a great wall of stone or iron." Her friend Dovey Johnson Roundtree was also familiar with the term. "Even now" Roundtree added, a half century later, "the phrase drags at my heart, as I remember how it felt to discover for the first time the impenetrable barrier between blacks and whites in the very place that stood for freedom and democracy."[133] And yet, despite its horrid racial caste system, both Roundtree and Pitts found themselves drawn to the city. Roundtree expressed their conflicted emotions:

> Those who love Washington as I do will know ... not even cities in the Deep South, fragrant with blossoms ... quite match the springs of Washington, when even at dusk the pink and white of dogwood is visible against the marble of the monuments, softening the edges of a city that does its business with such seriousness. I often had the sense that Jim Crow hid himself better, there, than in other places, which made his appearance, as if out of nowhere, all the more painful.[134]

Pitts would have shared Roundtree's perception of the incongruity of the city's natural beauty and social ugliness: the former intensified the latter and made it even more harsh.

After the war, Lucia became even more determined to publish her work. In 1945, she joined Tomi Carolyn Tinsley, a former WAC and friend from Durham, North Carolina, and Helen C. Harris, a friend from Cambridge, Massachusetts, in coauthoring a book of poems, which they titled *Triad.* The volume was published by the Plymouth Press of Washington, DC, in December 1945. Harris, a government technician and graduate of Boston University and Durham's St. Augustine College, contributed twenty-eight poems, and Tinsley, who would earn a PhD in Physical Education from the University of Iowa and join the faculty at Florida A&M

University, twenty-five. Lucia contributed twenty-six, including several that she had written in Europe during the war; among the older pieces are the prizewinning "Let Them Come to Us," which she had entered in the American Negro Exposition of 1940.

The most innovative and original part of *Triad* is Pitts's modernist series, "Punctuation Suite." It features individual poems on elements of punctuation and grammar, such as "Semi-Colon," "Apostrophe," and "Period," which concludes the series. In July 1946, Dr. Nathaniel P. Tillman, chair of Atlanta University's English Department, reviewed *Triad* for *Opportunity* magazine. For him, "Of the three authors, Miss Pitts has the most sustained poetic quality." As evidence, he notes that "'The First Kiss' is a well-executed Shakespearean sonnet; and 'Transient,' with its single rhyme for each quatrain, is superb in its music." Tillman concludes his review, holding that "Miss Pitts's contributions end with 'Punctuation Suite,' a poetic orchestration that leaves no doubt of her ability as a poet."[135]

The following year, fresh off the publication of *Triad*, Pitts appeared on a panel with "women writers of the district." The event was sponsored by Delta Sigma Theta sorority in support of the National Council of Negro Women.[136] Others on the panel included Mary Church Terrell, whose 1940 autobiography *A Colored Woman in a White World* describes her early years in DC. A native of Memphis and graduate of Oberlin College, Church Terrell taught Latin in the 1890s at the city's legendary M Street School (later Dunbar High), where she met her husband, the Howard University–trained lawyer Judge Robert Terrell, who was the school's principal. She would go on to become a charter member of the NAACP and one of the country's leading civil rights activists. Her friend Beatrice Murphy was also present. Murphy's important poetry anthology *Negro Voices* (1938), which Pitts had helped to edit, as well as her subsequent volume, *Ebony Rhythm* (1948), gave voice to talented, though often unsung, African American poets, including Lucia Pitts.

In 1950, Lucia celebrated as her second cousin and an old neighbor from Bronzeville, World War II Navy veteran Charles Wilson Boyd Jr., received his law degree from DePaul University in Chicago. Boyd revealed in his important book, *Your Legacy from Thaddeus Stevens*, that Stevens, a US congressman and ardent abolitionist, was the "Real Emancipator," as opposed to Abraham Lincoln. Boyd's mother, Rozelle Ernest, was Lucia's cousin; she and her mother Katie had lived with Lucia and her mother in Chattanooga. Lucia kept in close touch with the family; she visited her Aunt Katie and cousin Rozelle in Cleveland in 1954 and again in 1960; Rozelle's grandson, attorney John F. Drewry, met Lucia in 1960 and remembers her as "a pleasant woman with dark glasses."[137] At his death in October 1990, Charles Boyd's obituary described him as "a quiet unassuming genius who became a lion in the courtroom when defending his own personal principles and those of his clients."[138]

By the 1950s, Pitts had undoubtedly resigned herself to the fact that she would never marry or have children. However, she had arranged a fulfilling personal life based on her increased work responsibilities, correspondence with friends from the WAC, church activities, and literary and cultural engagements. Her independence also enabled her to be an intrepid traveler. In "Fly the Wide Sky," published toward the end of her life, she urges others to join her, not merely for the adventure but because travel brings us closer to God:

> Your spirit finds no fulfillment
> Imprisoned in a tight-shut pod.
> Only in rising and going forth, in stretching our wings,
> Can we soar, soar high enough to reach God.

In 1954, Pitts realized her longtime dream to drive cross-country to California and back. Planning for the trip began in the early 1950s: she contacted dear friends from the 6888th Battalion and announced herself ready to accept their invitations to visit, and she solicited her contacts for companionship on the trip. She also carefully saved her leave until, by April 1954, she had accumulated thirty-eight days of leave and a small nest egg, which would eventually be supplemented by gifts from friends. Unfortunately, none of her friends had either the funds or the time to accompany her, so she determined to make the trip alone: "So it was that soon after five o'clock on Monday morning, April 19, I set my car in the direction of Virginia and zoomed away with growing exultation because at last I was making a dream come true."[139] Pitts describes herself on the trip as "a happy wanderer. Over mountains and waters, deserts and plains, I travelled 7,600 miles from Washington D.C., to Pasadena and San Francisco, Calif., to Chicago, and back to Washington. It was one of the most soul-satisfying things I ever did."[140]

In keeping with her lifelong mission of racial uplift, Pitts shared her trip with the African American community through the *Washington Afro-American,* a nationally read weekly newspaper. In an effort to encourage Black travelers at a time when automobile travel could have unpleasant consequences and many states and individual businesses still practiced Jim Crow, Pitts published an upbeat account of her adventure. After describing a terrifying tornado near Fort Worth, Texas, she breezily comments: "And what, after all, are a couple of brushes with weather over 7,600 miles and 38 days?"[141] Her response to racial incidents is similarly insouciant: they happen, yes, but should not prevent African Americans from exercising their right to geographic mobility. At the very end of the article, after experiencing thousands of miles of "ideal weather under clear skies" and "the wonder and magnificence ... of a glorious adventure," she acknowledges "a brush or two" with racial issues, but maintains they were "neither unexpected nor serious. ... Most rest-rooms were available without distinction; where I stopped at ice cream and snack stands, even in the South, my treatment was courteous."[142] The article in the *Afro-American* could be seen as a lightweight puff piece, but Lucia's intentions are deeply serious: African Americans should never relinquish their dreams and goals.

Although she became increasingly sidelined by arthritis, Lucia's travels were not over. In 1962, as typing became more difficult, she retired on disability; she had worked over twenty-five years with the US government, from 1933 to 1945 and from 1949 to 1962. Looking back, she reflected that "I have tried to do my part for my race quietly, but I hope effectively, by proving that a Negro could measure up in all the required ways and more."[143] To celebrate, she took a train to Harlem, visited her seventy-eight-year-old sister Lucille, and left New York on September 17 for a five-week air tour of Western Europe. She traveled to Switzerland, England, and France, where she visited old friends and reflected on her European tour of duty with the WACs. She arrived back in New York on October 25 and returned to Washington, DC.[144] During her final years in the city, she would bear witness to several landmark events, including the funeral of President John F. Kennedy and the 1963 March on Washington.

During this time, she also began writing her autobiography, tentatively titled *The Small Fire and How It Grew*. The first words were "The history of the Negro in the United States is being written in flaming letters these days." Clearly, she had collected and saved documents and correspondence for this purpose since the 1950s. By 1965, she had a manuscript of three hundred pages or 90,000 words. She sent the introduction, prologue, and chapter 1 to Dr. John Dizikes, a Harvard-educated assistant professor of history at the University of Connecticut. Dizikes, who would be a founding member of the new University of California at Santa Cruz, forwarded the manuscript to Dr. Leslie Fishel, director of the Wisconsin Historical Society. Fishel, a Harvard classmate of Dizikes, was an African Americanist; he edited several books with fellow historian Dr. Benjamin Quarles. Fishel in turn forwarded the manuscript to William Haygood, a former administrator of the Rosenwald Fund and editor of the Wisconsin Historical Society magazine.

Unfortunately, neither Fishel nor Haygood offered Pitts the slightest encouragement for publication, although they virtually salivated at the thought of getting their hands on her documents for the historical society. Fishel wrote a polite but condescending letter; he acknowledges that she "has a story to tell" and "fascinating anecdotes," but he objects to the fact that she conflates her "own narrative" with an account of "the Negro in the New Deal." He dislikes the impressionistic style and suggests a strict chronological order arranged "month by month, year by year." In a final insult, he proposes that she donate her unedited book to the manuscripts library of the historical society, "since it contains material not available elsewhere." Haygood is even more dismissive; in a private note to Fishel, he calls the manuscript "obviously unpublishable" and "studded with distracting amateurish devices," but he also wants the manuscript for the historical society where it would presumably be a resource for other historians. Haygood's review is even more baffling when one recalls his adulation of Chester Himes's violent and misogynistic novel *The Primitive* (1955). Clearly discouraged, Pitts made no further attempts at publication, although in the hands of a sympathetic editor, the manuscript would make a fascinating addition to African American women's history.[145]

In the mid-sixties Pitts decided to move to California; she had visited Los Angeles while stationed at Fort Huachuca, Arizona, and had fallen in love with the city. She may also have hoped the drier climate would improve her arthritis. On Saturday, May 1, 1965, with the last of her packing complete, Pitts moved across the country to Los Angeles. Initially, she lived with her friends Willis and Marie Montgomery, whom she had met in the 1930s in Washington, where Willis had worked for the government as a timekeeper. With their help, she found a perfect one bedroom, one bath house a block away from their elegant 2900 Stocker Plaza home. Although her Chicago roots would always remain close to the surface, Pitts would come to think of her residence at 4223 Garthwaite Avenue in Leimert Park, Los Angeles, as home.[146] At Garthwaite Avenue she spent much of her time writing her military memoir *One Negro WAC's Story*, probably at the urging of friends and WAC colleagues. The memoir, the most extensive firsthand account of the war effort written by a 6888th Battalion soldier, was privately published in 1968 and sold for $1.50 per copy.

Lucia's army pal Hazel Washington LaMarre was a prominent member of the African American community in Los Angeles and may have been instrumental in encouraging her friend's move. Born in 1908 in Kansas City, Missouri, Hazel Washington graduated from the University of Kansas, became a schoolteacher, and taught in the Kansas City suburbs before joining the WACs in January 1943 as an aviation cadet. She would eventually serve with Pitts in the 6888th Central Postal Directory Battalion.[147] After the war, she married Frenchman René Victor LaMarre, moved to California, and published two books of poems, *Breath in the Whirlwind* (1955) and *The Silence* (1972). When she and Lucia reconnected, LaMarre was writing a music column for the *Los Angeles Sentinel* and editing a column, "Writing on Poetry," for the *Southwest News*. It was in the latter capacity that she published a number of Lucia's "Los Angeles" poems.

Beginning in Chicago with "To My Flowers" (1925) and ending in Los Angeles with "Once Upon a Time" (1971), Lucia Pitts published energetically and successfully for nearly fifty years. Among the poetry's most prominent features is an essential air of optimism, likely stemming from her vivacious personality and her lived experience of struggle and success.

After her parents separated, Lucia and her mother moved from Chattanooga, Tennessee, to Chicago's Bronzeville, where she was raised in an extended family of ambitious and motivated strivers. She attended prestigious New Trier High School when her mother found work as a domestic on Chicago's affluent North Shore. After high school, Lucia herself worked as a "housemaid in a private home, and cue-girl in a down-town billiard parlor." "But finally," she stresses, "I got a foot on the rung of the ladder and, except for that depression period, gradually I begun to go a little higher."[148] The phrase "a little higher" reflects Pitts's characteristic modesty and self-deprecation: she went from housemaid to the highest rungs of governmental service that were available to a Black woman from the 1930s to the 1960s.

Any number of the poems are illustrative of Pitts's resilience in the face of adversity and determined optimism, though "This Is My Vow" and "Cockeyed Optimist" paint especially powerful portraits. In the former, the pleasure of wine functions as a controlling metaphor, as the speaker pledges: "This I have made my sacred vow: / The god of bitterness shall never be my god." Though she has known "pain and misery," even in death she will remember "only hours that made the happy years: / I will not spoil my piquant wine with bitter tears." "Cockeyed Optimist" is less figurative and more direct, as it uses self-deprecating humor to challenge convention. Set during the late 1960s and early 70s, with the Vietnam War raging abroad and demonstrations and protests intensifying at home, the cockeyed optimist announces plainly, "The world is in an awful mess / And problems everywhere abound." Yet the poem is ultimately optimistic: in acknowledging the "stars," "sunlight," and "flowers," she holds that mankind is "greatly blessed / With the mind and heart to make earth fair."

Religion, spirituality, and social responsibility undergird much of her verse. These values are evident in her life, from her teenage role as a church youth leader to her decision to join the armed forces and her later work as a Red Cross volunteer in Washington, DC and Los Angeles, and they are also manifest in her poetry.[149] For example, selflessness, love of country, and concern for the race lie at the heart of "A WAC Speaks to a Soldier"; the poem's speaker personally sacrifices for her country and empathetically sees the perspective of male soldiers marching off to war: "We send you forth, / And as you go marching in never-ending files, / With our hearts and the work of our hands / We salute you."

Lucia Pitts continued writing poetry until the end of her life. In the winter of 1971, she published her last poem, "Once Upon a Time," in *The Southwest Wave*. Its deceptively upbeat, celebratory tone captures her positive, unassuming personality and seems to presage her own passing. The speaker, clearly Pitts, offers a sustained reflection on her loves, beginning with young love, when "There were birds singing and bells ringing, / And exquisite pain, and ecstasy." But that was "a long ago"; now she can "cherish memories of those days; / On long evenings it is pleasant to reminisce / And give them due praise." She concludes on a buoyant note: "But no pity for me, I implore. / . . . I am so glad at last to be free / And to belong only to me!"

Lucia Pitts died in Los Angeles, California, on December 17, 1973, a month before her seventieth birthday. She was survived by her brothers Harrison William Pitts and Edgar Jaques Pitts, both of Chicago, and her sister Lucille Pitts Langston of New York City. Her brothers arranged a memorial service in Chicago; federal employees also organized a service in Washington, DC, where she had labored for many years. Although Pitts never married or had children, her legacy is a body of poetry that captures a remarkable African American life.

Notes

1. "Letter to the Editor," *Chicago Defender*, January 23, 1932, 15.
2. Mary E. Stovall, "*The Chicago Defender* in the Progressive Era," *Illinois Historical Journal* 83. 3 (1990), 160.
3. Early contributors to the column who are now relatively well known include Frank Marshall Davis, Langston Hughes, Countee Cullen, Georgia Douglas Johnson, Clarissa Scott Delany, Anita Scott Coleman, John Henrik Clarke, and Gwendolyn Brooks.

4. Lucia M. Pitts, *One Negro WAC's Story* (1968), 1.
5. For detailed information on African American women in the military, including the social geography of military installations for Black women stationed at Forts Des Moines, Huachuca, and Oglethorpe, see Mattie E. Treadwell's two-volume history, *The Women's Army Corps: United States Army in World War II* ([1954], 2016); Charity Adams Earley's memoir *One Woman's Army: A Black Officer Remembers the WAC* (1989); Brenda Moore's *To Serve My Country, To Serve My Race* (1996); and Martha S. Putney's *When the Nation Was in Need: Blacks in the Women's Army Corps During WWII* (1992). See also Pauline Peretz's 2022 work on Fort Huachuca, *Une armée noire: Fort Huachuca, Arizona (1941–1945)*, forthcoming in English from Cambridge University Press in 2025.
6. Samantha Ege, "The Curious Case of a Shape Shifter of the Jazz Age," *New York Times*, November 17, 2024, arts section, 6–7. See also Ege's *South Side Impresarios: How Race Women Transformed Chicago's Classical Music Scene* (2024).
7. Brenda L. Moore, in her excellent history of the 6888th Battalion, *To Serve My Country, To Serve My Race*, draws extensively on Pitts's account of life for the WACs in Birmingham, Rouen, and Paris.
8. Angela Y. Davis, *Blues Legacies and Black Feminism: Gertrude "Ma" Rainey, Bessie Smith, and Billie Holiday* (1999), xv.
9. "Chicago Commercial Institute," *Chicago Whip*, February 5, 1921, 3.
10. John S. Burger, "Annabel Carey-Prescott: African American Educator and Chicago Leader," *Journal of the Illinois State Historical Society* 112. 2 (2019), 194.
11. Burger, "Annabel Carey-Prescott," 194.
12. Anne Innis Dagg, *Mary Quayle Innis: The Woman Who Inspired Me* (2021), 5; D. D. Robbins, "Mary Quayle Innis," *Salem Press Biographical Encyclopedia* (2023).
13. Lucia M. Pitts, *The Little Fire and How It Grew*, section 4, 20–21 (1981); *New Trier Echoes*, 18. 4 (1920), 11, 17.
14. Dorothy West, "The Gift," in *The Richer, the Poorer* (1995), 177.
15. Harriet Monroe, "News Notes," *Poetry* 30. 5 (1927), 298.
16. All issues of *Poetry* magazine have been digitized at PoetryFoundation. org, https:// www. poetryfoundation. org/poetrymagazine/archive.
17. Cheryl A. Wall, "Nora Holt: New Negro Composer and Jazz Age Goddess," in *Women and Migration: Responses in Art and History* (2019), 94.
18. Wall, "Nora Holt," 95.
19. Ege, "Curious Case of a Shape Shifter of the Jazz Age," 7.
20. Davis, *Blues Legacies and Black Feminism*, 319.
21. Davis, *Blues Legacies and Black Feminism*, 11.
22. William Henry Huff, "Happy New Year," *Chicago Defender*, December 28, 1935, 16.
23. Frank Marshall Davis, "Poetry by Eighty-Three Colored Writers," *Dayton Forum*, December 9, 1938, 4.
24. "Elizabeth Barrett," Massachusetts, US Marriage Records, 1840–1915; "Alonzo G. Long," Boston City Directory 1895, p. 884, both at Ancestry. com.
25. "Lucille W. Pitts," 1910 US Federal Census, Medford, Ward 6, Middlesex, MA; "Latin School Graduates," *Boston Post*, June 25, 1901, 6; "Lucille Langston," 1920 US Federal Census, Royal Oak, Oakland, MI; Application for Marriage License, State of Ohio, Greene County, Mr. Irving Y. Langston and Miss Lucille W. Pitts, May 5, 1917; "Sarah Barrett," "Lizzie Barrett," and "Willie Ann Barrett," 1870 US Federal Census,

Rome, Floyd, GA, all at Ancestry. com; see also "Marriage License Issued," *Xenia Daily Gazette,* May 8, 1917, 4.

26. "Jarrett Thomas Pitts, Jr.," US World War I Draft Registration Cards, 1917–18; "William H. Pitts," 1950 US Federal Census, Chicago, IL, both at Ancestry. com.
27. Jill Watts, *The Black Cabinet: The Untold Story of African Americans and Politics During the Age of Roosevelt,* (2020), 79; see also "Harrison Wm Pitts," US World War I Draft Registration Cards, 1917–18; "Jarrett T. Pitts," 1920 US Federal Census, Rome Ward 1, Floyd, GA; "Jane Pitts," 1920 US Federal Census, New Trier, Cook, IL, all at Ancestry. com.
28. Pitts, *One Negro WAC's Story,* 1.
29. "Frat President," *Detroit Tribune,* March 28, 1936, 1; "Royal Eugene Pitts," US Veterans Administration Master Index, 1917–40, Military Service, December 17, 1918, Roanoke, VA.
30. Moore, *To Serve My Country, To Serve My Race,* 17–18.
31. Moore, *To Serve My Country, To Serve My Race,* 135.
32. St. Edmund's Episcopal Church Archives, Vivian G. Harsh Research Collection of Afro-American History and Literature, Carter G. Woodson Regional Library, Chicago Public Library. See also "Thomas Pitts, Realtor, Dies," *Chicago Daily Defender,* November 6, 1961, 5.
33. "Frat President," *Detroit Tribune,* March 28, 1936, 1.
34. See "Frankie J. Muirhead," 1900 US Federal Census, Nashville, TN; "Frankie Price" and "Evlyn Muirhead," 1920 US Federal Census, Chicago, IL; "Royal Eugene Pitts and Frankie Price," Illinois, Cook County Marriages, 1871–1968, December 24, 1938, all at Ancestry. com.
35. By 1950, Edgar was the proprietor of his own interior decorating firm: see "Edgar J. Pitts," 1950 US Federal Census, Detroit, MI, Ancestry. com.
36. "Frat President," *Detroit Tribune,* March 28, 1936, 1; "Gaddings," *Michigan Chronicle,* March 3, 1945, 9; "Travelogue," *Detroit Tribune,* September 14, 1940, 5.
37. "Parade Plans Completed; Invite All," *Michigan Chronicle,* April 11, 1942, 4.
38. "Every Friday," *Chicago Bee,* December 2, 1945, 15; "Lil Palmore Star Attraction at Popular Pitts' Pub," *Chicago Bee,* January 20, 1946, 13.
39. Juanita M. Logan, "Lee Simons," *Chicago Bee,* February 10, 1946, 13; "On Discs," *Chicago Bee,* June 9, 1946, 15.
40. "Lucille Jones," Indiana, US Marriages, 1810–2001, July 12, 1927, p. 473, Film Number 002416334, Ancestry. com.
41. "St. Edmund's Banquet Sets Fanciful Mood of Gay Hawaii," *Chicago Defender,* May 17, 1958, 13.
42. "William H. Pitts," 1950 US Federal Census, Chicago, IL; "Lucille Pitts," 1930 US Federal Census, Chicago, IL, both at Ancestry. com; "Obituary for Ralph J. Pitts," *Chicago Tribune,* January 16, 1956, 71.
43. "Thomas Pitts, Realtor, Dies," *Chicago Daily Defender,* November 6, 1961, 5; "Obituary for Lois Searcy Pitts Bowles," *Chicago Sun-Times,* April 14, 2018.
44. "Searcy and Pitts Nuptials Season's Most Impressive," *Chicago Bee,* March 3, 1946, 9–10.
45. "Music Pageant," *Chicago Whip,* April 1, 1922, 5.
46. "Mrs. Janie Pitts Dies After Prolonged Illness," *Chicago Defender,* January 1, 1927, 5; "Lilliam Shaver," 1930 US Federal Census, New Trier, Cook, IL, Ancestry. com. In

1925, Pilgrim Baptist Church had the largest Black congregation in Chicago, with nearly six thousand members: see "Throng Attends Funeral for the Rev. S. E. J. Watson," *Chicago Tribune,* July 22, 1925, 12.
47. "James Hayes Honored," *Chicago Broad Axe,* October 13, 1923, 2.
48. Pitts, *Little Fire and How It Grew,* section 4, 20.
49. "Lucia Pitts Is Thoroughly Competent," *Pittsburgh Courier,* June 2, 1934, 8.
50. "Negro Girl Rated High as Steno at Ill. Capitol," *Negro World,* May 2, 1931, 2.
51. Hatch Himself, "Ah, If We Only Knew," *Chicago Defender,* December 3, 1927, A2.
52. Dewey R. Jones, "And Now It's Out," *Chicago Defender,* December 3, 1927, A2.
53. Lucia Pitts, "But Isn't It True?" *Chicago Defender,* December 17, 1927, 14.
54. Lucia Pitts to Horace Mann Bond, February 21, 1933, Horace Mann Bond Papers, Box 15, Folder 196, Special Collections and University Archives, University of Massachusetts Amherst.
55. The lyrics are from Pitts, "And We, We Fain. "
56. "Corrine Robinson" and "Lucia M. Pitts," 1930 US Federal Census, Chicago, IL, Ancestry. com.
57. "Negro Girl Rated High as Steno. at Ill. Capitol," *Negro World,* May 2, 1931, 2.
58. Cecilia Goldsby, "Soldiers Will Be Gentlemen If Met Half Way," *Apache Sentinel,* September 15, 1944, 4. The ellipses are in the original article.
59. "Letter to the Editor," *Chicago Defender,* January 23, 1932, 15.
60. Lady Lou, "We Are Getting Contributions," *Chicago Defender,* January 23, 1932, 15.
61. Lucia Pitts, "Sh—h! The Lady Called Lou Has an Idea," *Chicago Defender,* June 12, 1926, A2.
62. *Poetry* 30. 5 (1927): 295–98.
63. Frank Marshall Davis, *Livin' the Blues: Memoirs of a Black Journalist and Poet* (1993), 117–18.
64. Pitts, *Little Fire and How It Grew,* "Prologue," 8.
65. Pitts, *Little Fire and How It Grew,* "Prologue," 8.
66. "Negro Girl Rated High," *Negro World,* 2.
67. "Expert Stenog," *Pittsburgh Courier,* July 25, 1931, 1.
68. Pitts, *Little Fire and How It Grew,* "Prologue," 8.
69. Pitts, *Little Fire and How It Grew,* "Prologue," 6–7.
70. Pitts, *Little Fire and How It Grew,* "Prologue," 7.
71. Pitts, *Little Fire and How It Grew,* "Prologue," 7.
72. Pitts, *Little Fire and How It Grew,* "Prologue," 7.
73. Pitts, *Little Fire and How It Grew,* "Prologue," 7.
74. Vivian Ferguson, "It's News to Me," *News-Journal* (Mansfield, OH), April 29, 1951, 30.
75. "Pitts Is Thoroughly Competent," *Pittsburgh Courier,* June 2, 1934, 8.
76. Dorothy West, "Elephants Dance: A Memoir of Wallace Thurman," in *Where the Wild Grape Grows,* ed. Verner D. Mitchell and Cynthia Davis (2005), 167.
77. West, "Elephants Dance," 173.
78. West, "Elephants Dance," 168.
79. "Miss Lucia Pitts Appointed Secretary to Clark Foreman," *Washington Tribune,* September 7, 1933, 5.
80. Interview with Clark Foreman, November 16, 1974, 23–24, University of North Carolina Southern Oral History Program Collection. https://docsouth. unc. edu

/sohp/B-0003/B-0003. html. Also see Clark Foreman, "Decade of Hope," *Phylon* 12. 2 (1951), 139; and "Pitts Appointed Secretary to Foreman," *Washington Tribune*, September 7, 1933, 5.
81. Beatrice M. Murphy, preface to *Negro Voices: An Anthology of Contemporary Verse* (1938), 5.
82. Murphy, preface to *Negro Voices*, 5–6.
83. Murphy, acknowledgments to *Negro Voices*, 2.
84. Davis, "'Negro Voices': Poetry by Eighty-Three Colored Writers," 22.
85. Davis, "'Negro Voices': Poetry by Eighty-Three Colored Writers," 22.
86. After retiring to California, Pitts found her Red Cross volunteer work "a wonderful way to learn about Los Angeles and at the same time be doing something worthwhile. " See "Red Cross Seeks Drivers," *Evening Vanguard* (Venice, CA), July 13, 1966, 16.
87. The Eva Jessye choir, which would later sing at the 1963 March on Washington, was among the groups that performed for Pitts's music hour concert series. See "Music Hour Series," *Evening Star* (Washington, DC), December 11, 1934, C-8.
88. "Government Group in Monthly Meeting," *Chicago Defender*, March 11, 1939, 14.
89. Anderson sang at Pilgrim Baptist, as a soloist, in June 1922 and again in January 1923. See Nora Douglas Holt, "News of the Music World," *Chicago Defender*, May 13, 1922, 5; and Holt, "Umbrian Glee Club Presents Fine Program: Miss Marion Anderson . . . ," *Chicago Defender*, February 3, 1923, 5.
90. Pitts, *Little Fire and How It Grew*, section 3, 2.
91. Pitts, *Little Fire and How It Grew*, section 4, 21.
92. Pitts traveled to New York to recruit Robinson, who was living in the city and recently working as an editor at the *Interstate Tattler*. While in New York, she also visited her sister, Lucille Langston, who had relocated there from Detroit: *Little Fire and How It Grew*, section 1, 21–22.
93. "Government Group in Monthly Meeting," *Chicago Defender*, March 11, 1939, 14.
94. "Corrine Kathleen Robinson" and "Edward Morrow," District of Columbia, US Marriage Records, 1810–1953; "Edward Morrow," US Veterans' Gravesites, ca. 1775–2019, both at Ancestry. com; Patricia Bell-Scott, *The Firebrand and the First Lady: Portrait of a Friendship—Pauli Murray, Eleanor Roosevelt, and the Struggle for Social Justice* (2016), 226. Morrow graduated from Yale in 1931 and was the only Black student in his graduating class.
95. "Government Personnel Form Organization," *Chicago Defender*, October 8, 1938, 14.
96. Lucia M. Pitts, "Written for Women," *Chicago Defender*, January 31, 1942, 15.
97. Cecilia Goldsby, "Orientation Notes from a Listener's Notebook," *Apache Sentinel*, July 21, 1944, 5; Lucia M. Pitts, "Employee Urges that U. S. Hire Able Negroes," *People's Voice*, August 29, 1942, 37; Lucia Mae Pitts, "The Back Streets of Business," *Pittsburgh Courier*, June 9, 1934, 8.
98. "Poetry Contest for American Negro Fair Won by Wiley Prof. ," *New York Age*, July 6, 1940, 4.
99. Walter B. Hill Jr. , "Finding Place for the Negro," *Prologue* magazine 37. 1 (2005).
100. Pitts, *One Negro WAC's Story*, 1. Named for Dr. Weaver, the Robert C. Weaver Federal Building is the headquarters of the US Department of Housing and Urban Development in Washington, DC.

101. Pitts, *One Negro WAC's Story*, 1.
102. "Jimcro Policy Stopped in Chicago US Treasury," *People's Voice*, December 19, 1942, 9.
103. "Lucia M. Pitts," US World War II Army Enlistment Records, 1938–46, Ancestry.com.
104. Pitts, *One Negro WAC's Story*, 3.
105. "Talented Pvt. Lucia Pitts Welcome Addition to WAC," *Apache Sentinel*, April 7, 1944, 7.
106. "Post Det. MPs Rate Highly in Arizona," *Apache Sentinel*, September 15, 1944, 4.
107. Pitts, *One Negro WAC's Story*, 5.
108. See "WACs Pick Pin-Up," *Apache Sentinel*, May 26, 1944, 2.
109. Pitts, *One Negro WAC's Story*, 6.
110. Pitts, *One Negro WAC's Story*, 6–7.
111. Some contend that the battalion was actually multiethnic, since one member was Puerto Rican and another Mexican. But of course, many Puerto Ricans and Mexicans are Black.
112. Pitts, *One Negro WAC's Story*, 9.
113. Pitts, *One Negro WAC's Story*, 17.
114. Pitts, *One Negro WAC's Story*, 11.
115. Pitts, *One Negro WAC's Story*, 16.
116. Moore, *To Serve My Country, To Serve My Race*, 4.
117. Company A was commanded First Lt. Berniece Gaines Henderson of Ohio; Company C by Capt. Vera A. Harrison of Ohio; and Company D by First Lt. Ella B. Tatum of Arkansas. There was also a Headquarters Company, commanded by Second Lt. Frances E. Flatts of New York: see Moore, *To Serve My Country, To Serve My Race*, 131.
118. Mandy Malone, "Vashi T. Willis, Last of Women's Auxiliary Corps," *Daily Press* (Newport News, VA), June 2000, Ancestry. com.
119. "S. Siders in 1st Negro WAC Unit to Go Overseas," *Chicago Tribune*, March 11, 1945, 2; Edward B. Toles, "First Wacs Overseas Greeted in Britain," *Chicago Defender*, February 24, 1945, 5. While stationed in France, Jacobs studied violin with Mme. Talluell at the Ecole de Musique in Paris. Richard C. Henderson, "Social Scene," *Indianapolis Recorder*, March 15, 1947, 4.
120. Sgt. Bernice Lockhart, "WACs and Facts," *Apache Sentinel*, September 24, 1943, 7.
121. "Novella Auls," US World War II Army Enlistment Records, 1938–46, Ancestry. com.
122. "Huachuca WACs Score Cage Win," *Arizona Daily Star*, March 5, 1944, 13; "Two Cincinnati WACs," *Cincinnati Post*, June 29, 1955, 9; "356th Inf. Wins," *Apache Sentinel*, August 11, 1944, 8.
123. Moore, *To Serve My Country, To Serve My Race*, 128. Auls and Cruse were teammates on the Fort Huachuca basketball team. See "'High' Girls Lose 3rd Game to WACs After First Half," *Apache Sentinel*, March 3, 1944, 6.
124. In 1989, as she was hospitalized with her final illness, colon cancer, Novella Auls summoned a Hampton University professor to her bedside, gave her a copy of Lucia Pitts's *One Negro WAC's Story*, and asked that she use it to tell her story and that of the 6888th. *Flaming Letters* aims to fulfill, at least in part, Sergeant Auls's request. See Margaret Bristow, "Hear About Hampton Woman Who Served in WWII Black Women's Battalion in WWII," City of Hampton, YouTube, March 16, 2018.

125. Pitts, *One Negro WAC's Story,* 20, 22.
126. Pitts, *Little Fire and How It Grew,* section 6, 50d.
127. "Capital to Get Personal Service Bureau," *Chicago Bee,* June 23, 1946, 3.
128. Pitts, *Little Fire and How It Grew,* section 1, 22, and section 6, 50.
129. "Lucia Pitts, Government's Talented Intergroup Officer," *Pittsburgh Courier,* February 24, 1962, 28.
130. "Planning Committee for SWO [Service Women's Organization] Thru WACs," *Alabama Tribune,* August 1, 1947, 2; Pitts, *One Negro WAC's Story,* 20, 22; Pitts, *Little Fire and How It Grew,* section 3, 19.
131. Dovey Johnson Roundtree and Katie McCabe, *Mighty Justice: My Life in Civil Rights* (2019), 41–43.
132. Roundtree and McCabe, *Mighty Justice: My Life in Civil Rights,* 27.
133. Roundtree and McCabe, *Mighty Justice: My Life in Civil Rights,* 43–44.
134. Roundtree and McCabe, *Mighty Justice: My Life in Civil Rights,* 112.
135. N. P. Tillman, "A Book of Lyric Poetry" [Review of *Triad*], *Opportunity* 24. 3 (1946): 159–60.
136. "Deltas Present First Gift for NCNW 'Woman's Museum,'" *Daily Bulletin,* July 16, 1946, 2.
137. John "Jack" Drewry, telephone interview with the volume editors, May 7, 2024.
138. "Obituary for Charles W. Boyd," *Atlanta Constitution,* October 18, 1990, 51.
139. Lucia M. Pitts, "Around the U. S. in 38 Days," *Washington Afro-American,* magazine section, August 24, 1954, 1.
140. Pitts, "Around the U. S. in 38 Days," 1.
141. Pitts, "Around the U. S. in 38 Days," 6.
142. Pitts, "Around the U. S. in 38 Days," 6.
143. Pitts, *Little Fire and How It Grew,* section 5, 17.
144. "New York Beat," *Jet* magazine, October 14, 1962, 63. See also "Lucia M. Pitts," New York State Passenger and Crew Lists, 1917–67, Ancestry. com, showing that she flew from Zurich to New York.
145. Letters from Dizikes, Fishel, and Haygood are filed with the Pitts manuscript at the Wisconsin State Historical Society.
146. "Willis C. Montgomery," Los Angeles City Directory, April 1967; "Willis C. Montgomery" and "Marie Henrietta Montgomery," 1950 US Federal Census, Detroit, MI, all at Ancestry. com; Lucia M. Pitts Membership Card, All Souls Church, Washington, DC, courtesy of Barbara Corprew.
147. "Hazel L. Washington," US World War II Army Enlistment Records, 1938–46, Ancestry. com; "Obituary of Mrs. Rene V. LaMarre," *Kansas City Times,* October 10, 1973.
148. Pitts, *Little Fire and How It Grew,* section 4, 21.
149. See "Red Cross Seeks Drivers," *Evening Vanguard* (Venice, CA), July 13, 1966, 16.

One Negro WAC's Story

Lucia Pitts authored the following memoir after completing her tour of duty in the European Theater during World War II. Pitts served as a noncommissioned officer (NCO) in the US Army's 6888th Central Postal Directory Battalion in Birmingham, England, and Rouen, France.

The 6888th consisted of approximately 855 WACs (members of the Women's Army Corp), and it was the only all-Black, all-female battalion to serve overseas during the war. Because the unit was self-contained, members were responsible for all duties, including logistics, supply, recreation, vehicles, mess halls, military police, and mortuary services.

One Negro WAC's Story is the most extensive firsthand account of the war effort written by a 6888th Battalion soldier. It was privately published in Los Angeles in 1968 and sold for $1.50 per copy.

When the Women's Army Auxiliary Corps came into being in May of 1942, I wanted to dash right out and be among the first to join up. But I was then working as Administrative Assistant for Robert Weaver in one of the defense agencies of the Federal Government in Washington and, idiot that I was, I let him convince me that his office needed me more than the

WAAC did. I was an idiot because I left that job anyway before the end of the year and moved to another in Chicago.

Well, I didn't have to take that Chicago job, did I? If I was so all-fired anxious, why didn't I join the WAAC instead? I didn't because I felt I owed it to my race to take the job. The Treasury Department's Bureau of Public Debt in Chicago had been under heavy fire for its segregationist policies; it had decided to straighten up and fly right and its initial step in this direction was to employ its first Negro personnel official, who would be mainly responsible for the change-over. From a list of potentials I had been selected and offered the job. Having most of my working life been a racial guinea pig, and having been attempting in a quiet way to show that Negroes could measure up, I felt I could not miss this opportunity to strike another blow. So it was not until I felt I had done my job at the Bureau, after ten months, that on a cold winter's morning in December of 1943 I slipped out of the house in Chicago and finally offered myself to the Army of the U.S. Even then I was still going against the wishes of others—against my oldest brother Roy (that was why I had to slip out of the house), and against some friends. Roy never told me exactly why, but I suspect he had heard and believed the scurrilous rumors that the WACs (the "Auxiliary" was soon dropped) were only in the Army for the "entertainment" of the soldiers, and he was therefore dead set against my becoming one of them. (I don't recall that my other brothers—Edgar, Harrison and Ralph—felt the same way.) My friends argued that I was too independent and too used to giving orders to be able to take them. I went against them all and found them all wrong. The WACs were in the Army to work—to replace men at all possible non-combat jobs and thereby release the men for combat, and you can believe that we did indeed WORK. Oh, yes—there were a few who got in with entertainment in mind, but take it from me, they were quietly weeded out and sent packing. As for my taking orders, I took them as all the other girls did, though in my assignments I also continued to give some. It was fated, I think, that I become a WAC; for all along the way there were too many obstacles which had to be overcome (over and above those in the way of just signing up) and miraculously were. First off, I passed the physical exam despite bad nerves and what one examining physician said was an inward goitre. The miracle here was emphasized in my mind by the fact that the girl in line in front of me, who looked as if she didn't know what a nerve was, was turned down because of them; but Nervous Nellie me was accepted. As for the goitre, I had to be sent to the head physician for special permission to be accepted, and he gave it. Just before Christmas, orders came for me to report for active duty January 14, 1944, and, with some other Negro enlistees (the Services were then racially segregated) I was sent to Fort Des Moines, Iowa, for basic training. What a new adventure! All the Army trappings and uniforms on Post, the precise schedules for tests and classes and drilling and clean-up chores (Police the area! Scrub the floors! And on and on. . . .) the hurry-up-and-wait, the wonders of the PX, living in barracks with lots of others, reveille, drill, bathing in communal bathrooms with no privacy, white glove inspection, Mess Hall, the utter exhaustion at the end of the day when we would come in barracks and get no farther than the footlockers at the ends of our beds before we collapsed; lights-out, taps. . . . For me—and for all of us, I'm sure—it was an entirely new world and a somewhat overwhelming one.

One memory from my early days at Des Moines stands out. When I arrived on Post they were hard put to supply proper uniforms and I was given an outsize man's overcoat with some men's boots. The following Sunday, strolling around the grounds with some buddies, I ran into Beatrice Robinson, a friend from Washington who had enlisted before me and arrived in Des Moines ahead of me. She was trim and immaculate in her well-fitting uniform—and there I was, lumbering along in my big boots and ill-fitting overcoat. Bea stared at me and asked, "Lucia, is that *you?*" I wished I could just fade away.

After about three weeks in Des Moines, I was awakened one night by the CQ, who came to tell me my brother Roy was ill and the Red Cross had arranged for me to entrain to Chicago immediately. I had to borrow a decent uniform, dash to Officers' Quarters to get my papers signed, and then on to the railroad station to catch the next train.

My brother had had a stroke and doctors were not sure he would live. I'm fairly certain his worry over me helped bring on the stroke, especially since, when I arrived, he apparently thought I was there to stay and managed to get out the words—"I got you out of there, didn't I?"

But Roy pulled through (and lived many more active years); so, after my ten-day furlough was up, I reported back to Des Moines. There I found my company had had its final tests and was packing to move to the staging area (for the uninitiated, this was the ready-to-move-out-to-another-station area), being on orders for permanent assignments in the field somewhere, we knew not where.

And once again an obstacle was overcome. Before I had been called back from Chicago, another girl had had to go home on emergency leave, and on her return to the Post had to start her training all over again with another company. I thought I would have to do the same, but not so; I was on orders, too. Immediately after I reported in, I was rushed to examinations which I took alone, miraculously passed despite having missed many classes, and moved with my company to the staging area that night. Within five days we entrained—all of us for Arizona, but I alone for Fort Huachuca, the others for Douglas. (I never learned why I alone was sent to Fort Huachuca.)

Arriving in the utter quiet and deep dark of late night at Hereford, Arizona, I was met at the station by a car and spirited away to the WAC area of Fort Huachuca where the CQ for WAC Section SCU 1922 assigned me to a temporary bed in one of the barracks. When I walked in, one of the girls—supposedly asleep, because it was 'way after lights out'—rose up and announced, "New WAC!"—whereupon all the others sat up in their beds to look me over and ask questions. (This was something different; new assignees did not usually arrive in the dead of night.)

Next morning all the girls hurried through their morning routine and off to their work assignments. Not knowing what else to do, I just sat beside my cot in the quiet and aloneness of empty barracks, waiting for something to happen. After a while Lt. Violet Askins, WAC Executive Officer, came through on her inspection tour and delivered me to the Commanding Officer, Lt. Irma Cayton. I was then assigned to permanent living quarters in Barracks 1966. (Let this go down in history, barrack-mates Kelly, Taylor, Auls, Johnson, Lewis, Hughes, Robeson, Gates, Littlejohn, Dawson, DeFreese, Cheatham, Hand, Watts, Bracey, Jones, Christian, and Little Sarges Linzey and Ward.)

Our Cpl. Bracey, incidentally, had a favorite saying which came to be adopted by all of us and which pretty well reveals the WAC philosophy: "I am not afraid of tomorrow, for I have seen yesterday and I love today."

Fort Huachuca was the largest Negro military installation in the world, covering a vast expanse of space nestled beneath high mountains, near Tucson and not far from Nogales, the Mexican border town. In addition to administrative and hospital buildings, countless men's barracks and a lesser number of women's barracks in the isolated WAC area, the scattered facilities included three indoor theaters and one open-air, a bowling alley, the Red Cross building, service clubs, officers' clubs, guest houses, Chapel, restaurants, swimming pools, and, of course, acres of open fields for drills and other training.

The first contingent of WACs—the first, white or colored, to be assigned to any Post—had arrived at Huachuca in December of 1942, to be greeted by Col. Edwin N. Hardy, Post Commander (white, of course) and the resident 93rd Infantry. They (we, that is) came to be known as "Colonel Hardy's WACs"—not just because we were under his command but mainly because he seemed to love us so—and the best WAC installation in the Ninth Service Command.

Women had come to Huachuca, after their basic training elsewhere, from practically everywhere; they had been clerks, stenographers, chauffeurs, truck drivers, bookkeepers, librarians, photographic assistants, switchboard operators, water and sewage analysts, map makers, cooks, butchers, artists, postal workers, musicians, public relations workers, teletype operators, finger-printers. And they did all their jobs so well that Col. Hardy proudly told the world, "I do not believe that there is a station in the United States Army where the WACs have proven of greater value than they have at Fort Huachuca." To go into detail about the WAC days at Fort Huachuca would be to do a book on just that; so let me just touch on what were some high spots for me.

My working assignment was with the Post Provost Marshal, Major J. J. Vincent (also white, of course), where I understudied and eventually replaced the male Sergeant Major. The Provost Marshal and his men comprised the police force for the Post, and my work as Acting Sergeant Major involved administering and supervising all the office work and other clerks, as well as some say over about 150 MPs. This meant devising methods and procedures, establishing and supervising a new filing system covering administration, law infractions, fingerprints, prisoners, etc., and handling all correspondence, reports and such. Sometimes I accompanied Major Vincent on his investigations to take notes. I got into other things, too. Soon after my arrival the *Apache Sentinel,* the Post paper, carried my photograph and a story about me. Two of my poems were run in the *Sentinel* later, and just before one of the battalions was to move out, by request I went to its area and read for them one of the poems, "A WAC Speaks to a Soldier," over the loudspeaker system.

Langston Hughes was one of the celebrities who visited on the Post, and flattered me by looking me up, when I was sure he wouldn't remember me, and autographing a copy of his poem, "The Negro Mother," for me. I got a five-day pass to make my first visit to Los Angeles and it made a lasting impression. (Later, I came back again and again, and I write this from my newly established home there.) I was once the principal speaker at chapel services conducted by the WAC section.

Through one friend, I found another in Tucson, Arizona, and used to go there often on holidays and weekends, travelling the route most of the time in a battered old car I had bought off an overseas-bound soldier for $125.

My working boss, Major Vincent, got tired of my having to be absent once a month for KP duty, required of all Privates and PFCs, so he instituted steps for my promotion. My CO refused to go along, saying I had been there too short a time, and the other girls had been waiting much longer for promotions. Major Vincent thereupon went over her head to the Post Commander, who decreed that I should be promoted to T/5 (comparable to Corporal) at once, and to T/4 (Sergeant) within 90 days. And so it was. In time, two of my special assignments made me a member of the WAC Orientation Council, and WAC reporter for the Post paper, the *Apache Sentinel.* In the former capacity I participated in planning regular orientation class activities and once prepared a script called *The Negro* for presentation in the WAC area—sung, danced and acted out by my sister WACs with the assistance of the 29th Special Service Company. At a second presentation at the Lena Horne open-air theater, ordered by Colonel Hardy, some pretty important people participated. They included Dr.

(Colonel) Midion O. Bousfield, Harry Mills of the Mills Brothers, Chaplain Granville Martin, singer-actors Babe Wallace and Lawrene Whisonant, artist Eugene Harper Johnson, and the Post Special Services Band under Cpl. Lloyd Pinkey, formerly of the Columbia Broadcasting System. WAC participants were Phyllis Branch, Novella Auls, Olive Dedeaux, Glenn Edward, Della Haney, Elva Poole, Grace Simpson, Pauline Small.

I took the written examination for Officer Candidate School and flunked it. But practically everybody else flunked, too; so it was decided by our officers that the circumstances must have been against us (we took the exam in the Mess Hall, where there were constant loud noises and many interruptions from both within and without) so the exam was repeated under more favorable conditions. This time I passed, along with a few others, and we were scheduled next for our orals. Meantime, rumors had been going the rounds that we were all to be shipped overseas. But rumors on Army posts are rife and frequently wrong, so we put little faith in this one until in December of 1944 several of us were asked if we'd care to volunteer for overseas duty. Ten of us answered yes—but I had to choose between OCS and overseas and, after I had chosen the latter, they had to get special permission from Washington for me, immediately granted, because I was over age. (Another obstacle overcome!)

Then we were rushed through physicals and other processing, were honored at a special dinner in the Mess Hall that Sunday, extolled by a proud Col. Hardy, and presented Good Conduct medals. Monday morning, serenaded by the Post band, we were escorted by Col. Hardy, Lt. Consuela Bland (who had replaced Lt. Cayton as our CO), and a great many others, to the bus which would take us to the railroad station in Hereford for overseas furloughs at home, happily coming at Christmastime. In our historic group, besides me, were Pvt. Charlotte Cartwright, PFCs Dorothy Reid, Marie B. Gillisslee, Mildred Gates; T/5s Edna Burton, Alice Allison, Fannie Talbert; T/4s Evelyn C. Martin and Mildred Peterson. According to the reports, we were selected because of our "character and capability," and we were the very first Negro WACs to volunteer for and be assigned to overseas stations. Immediately after the furlough, we reported at Fort Oglethorpe, Ga., and were put through intensive training, including a five-mile hike in full regalia (pistol belts, gas masks, canteens, packs and helmets) under active war conditions, learning how to climb up and down a cargo net, going through the gas chamber, in addition to a full day of classes, the usual cleaning details, caring for our own furnaces, KP, and doing on our own personal washing, ironing and cleaning. And if you think Georgia is a warm state, you should have been in our barracks those early January mornings when the fire in the furnace had gone out and, shivering mightily, we had to get it going.

My experience with the cargo net might have cost me my trip abroad. I went up and came back down in approved fashion but, jumping off, landed flat-footed. This gave my spine a painful jolt but I tried to shrug it off and mentioned it to no one for fear something would be found so wrong with me they'd cancel my overseas orders. The pain became increasingly unbearable, however, and finally I told my bunkmate about it. Every night thereafter, after lights-out, she and some others would sneak to my bunk and give me the "treatment"—rubs, hot water bottle and the works. With this I was able to hold out.

A never-before-tried responsibility somehow got to be mine at Oglethorpe: I became director of our Company choir, one of those singing at chapel services. How it happened I do not remember; I do know that, though I had consorted a lot with musicians and once did some singing, I am not a musician. But the choir got many compliments and my assignment stuck throughout our stay in England.

On a Saturday, the last of January, the 500 of us then assembled at Oglethorpe (WACs had been coming in from everywhere) were told to pack our duffle bags and get them outside. Sunday morning we were marched to the rail center where we boarded a special train which got us to Camp Shanks, New York, Monday afternoon. At Shanks—where it was miserably cold—we stayed for five days for final processing, and were heart-broken because we had already been alerted—which meant no telephone calls, no trips off Post. But a noble effort was made to entertain us during our little free time, with a dance and several shows at which Joe Louis and Ethel Merman, among others, appeared. Colonel Hobby, head of the WAC, came to bid us bon voyage; Public Relations wrote innumerable stories and took countless pictures. And we came near freezing, standing in formation outside while being taught how to line up for our ship in passenger list order.

Friday afternoon we successfully got ourselves in that passenger list order—helmets, packs, and all, and boarded a train which took us to a ferry, which took us to the dock where we were to board our ship. Chilled to the bone, we certainly welcomed the hot coffee and doughnuts the Red Cross served while we were waiting to embark; and to try and forget how cold we were—as well as keep up our spirits—we sang and sang and sang. (WACs burst into song anytime, anywhere—at least they used to.)

Eventually the great moment arrived and we trudged up the gangplank to a ship shrouded in darkness, singing out our first names after the Sergeant called the last names and then checked us off the list. We were guided immediately to our staterooms (staterooms?!) without then knowing the name of the ship (it was the *Ile de France,* we learned later), what it looked like, or where we were headed. And we had no opportunity for a dramatic farewell to the States; we were ordered to remain in our rooms and go to bed. The next morning, when we awakened, the liner had pulled off and we were at sea, with nothing around us but water, water, and more water.

Thus, on February 3, 1945, there was this historic first: Unknown by our families and friends, a contingent of Negro WACs, including me, was headed for somewhere overseas where the shooting war was.

After we were on the water, I reported for sick call and, as a result, all the way over was wrapped in adhesive tape—a corset of it about eight inches wide. But I was on the ship!

Compared to the accommodations of the men who slept in tiers in the hold of the ship, the WACs were well off. Still, there were twenty of us and more in each stateroom, sleeping in double bunks, and we were so crowded we did our dressing and undressing in our beds. The food we ate in the hot, dank hold, after standing in line for perhaps half an hour, was pretty awful. We had no recreational facilities; we were allowed on deck only at certain times; and smoking was permitted on deck (in the day, never in the dark) and in the latrine only. But church services were held regularly, and a variety show and movies helped to pass the time away.

The story is told—true or not—that our convoy could not accompany us all the way because our ship was too fast and that, consequently, in order to avoid detection and pursuit by submarines, the ship had to change its course every few knots. Because the water was rough in the first place and this constant changing of course did not make the sailing smoother, the ship rocked and rolled mightily. At times it seemed to be completely over on its side, almost tossing us out of our beds. We tried to be brave, but were frankly scared out of our wits and wore our life-belts most of the time, including while in bed. If anxious families ever doubted we knew how to pray, they should have been around then.

The rolling ship had another effect—it made numerous of our battalion, including our officers, sick unto death. Most of them stayed in bed and utterly miserable for most of the way over. Forgive me if I boast, but this *mal de mer* never struck me down. I went about being cheerful and active, and all the sick ones hated me.

This was the situation until February 11 when we awakened and wonder of wonders, found birds flying about us, ships at convoy, and—land! Everyone scrambled for a vantage point, on deck and at the portholes. The shoreline seemed all mountains for a time, many covered with snow; then buildings began to appear, some like little cottages and some like the old castles we'd read so much about.

The ship anchored that day but we were not to debark until the following morning. At that point we didn't mind. Land was in sight and all day we hung at the portholes getting a good look at it and waving to the sailors and fishermen passing by. On February 12 we set foot on Scottish soil and promptly boarded train for Birmingham, England. The picture of the Scottish and English countryside we got as the train sped along certainly lived up to its celebrated reputation and was a first impression never to be forgotten. The farmlands looked lush and green, but at intervals there was snow. Everything was laid out so neatly and precisely, with trim hedge-rows separating the plots, and little splashing falls here and there; and the land looked so clean it seemed it had been swept with a broom.

Although we arrived in Birmingham late at night, a large number of the Birmingham citizenry were on hand to observe and welcome us. We were the first American Negro women in uniform they had ever seen, and for some of them the first Negro women at all. Brigadier General B. O. Davis, the highest ranking Negro commissioned officer, officially welcomed us to England, and one of our first acts was to march to a big open field for a parade and inspection.

We were billeted in an old abandoned school house, somewhat the worse for wear. It had been quarters for soldiers before our coming, and they had used the walls for planning boards, as well as having knocked holes through them here and there. Nature had knocked a few holes in the roof. Our beds were double bunks which were so short they looked as if they had been made for children. Strips of tin were nailed across them for springs, and later, numerous cut fingers resulted from our trying to make tight beds, as ordered, while also fighting with the lumpy straw mattresses. But we did have sheets and pillows, and that was a boon.

The job of our battalion, the 6888th Central Postal Directory, was to keep up with the addresses of our fighting men, who were almost constantly on the move, and see that their mail reached them. Under the general command of Major Charity Adams, with Executive Officer Noel Campbell, and the working command of Captain Mary F. Kearney and Lt. Violet Hill, the WACs did a noteworthy job of cleaning out the backlog of letters and packages we found piled up like mountains when we arrived, then keeping up with those constantly arriving. An average of 30,000 address changes had to be made every day. I worked as administrative NCO for Captain Kearney and had to keep the records, so I know whereof I speak.

We worked under some trying circumstances, too. It was often so cold in the buildings that we had to bundle up like Eskimos and my fingers got so stiff with cold that I typed with gloves on.

It was hard, in the circumstances, to keep up with our standards of cleanliness; but we tried. When we could, we took baths in the laundry tubs or our showers in a building just outside, which we had to brave cold outside air, in our robes, to reach, and where the water was always either too hot or too cold and defied tempering. Failing to get tub or shower, we bathed in our helmets. (I got a gig once—demerit, to you civilians, for being in the laundry tub taking a bath when reveille was unexpectedly called and I couldn't make it.) Facilities for dry cleaning clothes not being so good, we washed everything but our overcoats, and a lot of it in our helmets. (Never think helmets are just made to be worn on the head!)

Our quarters required constant attention, also, being already in pretty bad shape. Every day, of course, we had to police our quarters enough to pass inspection; then at least once a week we'd get down on our knees and scrub. Before long a painting rash broke out, with WACs all over the place painting their rooms, hanging colorful curtains and making bedside tables and bookcases out of boxes we scrounged from here and there.

Delight was in time off, when we could see England, visit newly made friends, or attend the dances and shows and concerts.

I have spoken of the beauty of the Scottish landscape seen from a train window; I was even more awed by the English countryside, which I got to see at close range. It was the most restful, quiet and natural beauty imaginable—all trees, lush green grass, hedgerows and colorful flowers. Since we arrived at a time when the war was mainly being fought in France and up to Germany, we heard and saw little of it where we were; and in the loveliness and peace of the English countryside, with snug little cottages and big rambling estates all about, it was hard sometimes to realize there was a war going on. We were billeted in a good spot, with double-decker trams and busses at our front door. Five to fifteen minutes in either direction in front took us to the shops and cinemas and city; a turn to the back and we were in the beautiful country. We walked a great deal, went sight-seeing on the trams and busses, and frequented the Silver Birch Club, set up for us in quiet, restful surroundings by the British Women's Volunteer Services. And believe me, living and working in one building with over 700 women (more had come over after the first contingent), the need for peace and quiet was constant.

Of course we also frequented the pubs. The British pub is not like our taverns. They usually have several rooms instead of one big room, and always a "green" (lawn, to us) where the men bowl and, although they are not permitted inside, children play. To the British their daily ale is a tonic, not a means of getting drunk; and the pub is a place of general recreation. In most of the pubs I saw, there was no music or entertainment of any sort; but they were always crowded to the doors, so that if you arrived long after opening (they were open from 10 to 3 and 6 to 10), you literally plowed your way in and stood up or shared a seat with somebody who'd obligingly move over. But nobody cared that they were crowded. The English are supposed to be rather stuffy people, but they have fun. There was a contagious spirit of good comradeship about, and often everybody in the pub would be singing together. I stood in a group of British soldiers one night while one, with a haunting baritone, sang for me. In other corners other groups were singing, nobody minding anybody else.

The British welcomed us everywhere—to their pubs and theaters and churches and homes; and we were much made over. One English family, the Millenchips, sort of adopted my pal Ruth Jacobs and me and expected to see us at least one night a week at their favorite pub. If we didn't show up, they'd come looking for us to see if we were all right. And then, there was the Englishman who asked me to marry him and stay in England!

Our Negro soldiers in the area, incidentally, didn't care much for our hobnobbing with whites. One of them was so incensed over it that he slapped a WAC one night when he saw her going out with a white civilian. (And over in France, when a WAC friend and I were once out walking, a French sailor joined us. He was entirely respectful and, because of his knowledge of the area, added much to our understanding and enjoyment of the things around us. When he invited us into a café for a drink of wine, some Negro soldiers there tried to separate us from the sailor. When they did not succeed they became belligerent, followed us out and everywhere we went. We couldn't shake them off. By the grace of heaven, we were finally rescued by an Army vehicle which chanced down the street, bearing one of our WAC officers and my nephew—of whom more later.)

The British recognized the difference in our color but let it make no difference in their treatment of us. We were made to feel like people—not *colored* people; and it gave me great pride when one night an Englishman told me our manners would put theirs to shame. Another writer who did a feature story on us said the same thing about our English. Hear this

". . . They speak extremely good English—much better English than the average native. They have lively minds. . . . In fact, these WACs are very different from coloured women portrayed in the films, where they are usually either domestics or outspoken old-retainer type or sloe-eyed sirens given to gaudiness of costume and eccentricity in dress. The WACs have dignity and proper reserve.

Some of us got to London and other nearby cities on brief passes. To me it was like walking in a dream to see so many of the places about which I had read and heard for so long—Shakespeare's home at Stratford-on-Avon, Warwick Castle; and in London, Westminster Abbey, Big Ben and the Tower of London, 10 Downing Street, Piccadilly Circus, London Bridge, Scotland Yard, Buckingham Palace, Mme. Tussaud's famous wax museum, and so many such places.

The stories of some of the people gave insight into the apparent indestructability of the British.

On the train when we were on our way to London, a young British couple sat across from us in our compartment (he was on his way to "join up") and told us stories of the things they did during the air raids, laughing now at themselves. The girl related how she had gone to London one day wearing her very best suit, which had cost a lot of precious coupons and money. There was an air raid and she and her companion were unable to reach a shelter. The companion pushed her down on the ground not too tenderly, at which she protested violently because of the suit. When she dared to peek cautiously upward, detached human arms and legs were flying about her. She felt it entirely uncalled for when her companion said "Dash the bloody suit!"

One Sunday three of my WAC friends and I took a long bus ride, then got off and walked, following an enchanting lane. When we had tired, we looked for a bus stop and were waiting there when we spied a young English woman spading in her flower garden just behind us. Inquiring of her about the time the bus would arrive, she replied that it would be several minutes and invited us to come in and wait. We accepted the invitation and she showed us into a typically English bungalow, cool and restful and modern, with the usual fireplace in every room. Immediately she offered us tea, but we refused because of the stringent rationing which allowed little such hospitality.

We learned from our hostess that after she and her husband had been married about six months, he went off to the Royal Air Force. He had not been home then for nearly three years and had not yet seen their son, Michael.

Of course we got into a discussion of air raids. Our hostess said there had not been any recently; but when the baby was small they had been very bad. Still, she felt, they had been very lucky. One night she came out of the shelter, the baby in her arms, to find the fields across from her a sheet of flame, and a bit of her roof and a window or two of her house had been hit. But they were still alive and England had not been conquered. That was what mattered. "It isn't the exploding of the bombs that you mind so much after a bit," she reflected. "It's waiting for them to fall. You hear them start down with that whistling whine, and then there's nothing you can do but wait tensely and hold your breath until they hit. When they do finally hit, you feel a kind of relief."

There were other stories of this sort, and I could not help but admire the people who had endured so stoically and bravely, with such good humor, the horrors and deprivations of real war. And though it was quiet when we were there, evidence of the war was still to be seen. It wasn't pretty.

When we were standing at parade rest at reveille one morning, a little more than two months after we arrived in England, the Sergeant said to us: "We have just been informed of the death of President Roosevelt."

We stood there in utter silence, not believing we rightly heard what had been said. Then someone burst out—foolishly, not knowing what to say but having to say something—"You're kidding!"

The Sergeant reproached her: "Do you think I'd kid about something like that?"

We continued to stand there, stunned. I remember finally stamping my foot and saying out loud, "Oh, no!" Some girls openly wept. The Sergeant announced a memorial retreat for the next day and dismissed us. We wandered blindly away, the usual high spirits and chit-chat missing.

It was an altogether sad, mournful day. All the world had suffered a great loss but we, being Negroes, felt we had lost more than most—the first President in the lifetime of many of us who had seemed to care about us. It hit me even harder, I think, for while I had never met the President in person, I had been a small part of his early efforts and naturally felt a closeness and loss I believe others could not feel.

FDR needed no words from me—they were pouring out from others all over the world; but I wrote some, just the same, and my Commanding Officer posted them on the bulletin board as our Company's tribute.

I remember well the memorial retreat, the sound of taps falling mournfully upon the stillness and more than usually sending shivers up my spine, while all our eyes were front and riveted against our will on the flag at half-staff.

For us, as for all, the burden of grief lightened with time, but we will never forget the impact of it then, nor will we forget him or the dauntless and beloved Eleanor Roosevelt who has now gone to join him.

The life we still had to live got a good shot in the arm with the news of V-E Day in May. Hilarious delight was mixed with deep thanksgiving and sorrow, too. When we were dismissed from work for the holiday, we went immediately to our Rec Hall where a young British minister led us in a service of thanksgiving. That night, and for several after, on the streets and in the pubs there was dancing and singing and gaiety; but there were tears, too, for FDR and all those others who had not lived to see the day. The following Sunday Birmingham had a great victory celebration. A hundred volunteers from our battalion represented the American armed forces in the parade, and perhaps it was just *esprit de corps,* but I thought they were the about the snappiest, best-looking outfit there.

While we were in England, too, we celebrated the third anniversary of the WAC. Ours was in the form of a pantomime depicting the WAC from its official organization to our battalion's coming to England. I was good-naturedly dunned by Captain Mildred Carter, to prepare this pantomime; and I suppose I should feel honored that she considered me good enough to do the job in one night. Right then I said things about her I don't even now dare repeat.

My choir was still a feature of our battalion, too. I had written words and melody for a song, "Salute to Britain," which my friend Ruth Jacobs arranged, and my singing group became the first WACs to appear before a British audience when we sang it and other numbers for a group which had requested us. Also, my Commanding Officer, Lt. Vashti Tonkins, drafted me to help with the chapel service when our Company B was in charge, and the choir under my direction.

After we had been in England about three months, news came that we were to move on to France; and very early one Sunday morning, again in full packs and other regalia, we were routed to a train which took us to Southampton port and a small ship. On this boat we slept sailor fashion—in our clothes, on pieces of canvas that let down from the wall shelf-fashion. Nothing was on these shelves but us, our life belts, and our overcoats for covering. Since we slept in tiers of four to six, if you lifted your head from your bunk without thinking, you popped it against the bunk above you; and if you leaned over the side without care you were likely to bump the head of the person beneath you. And on this ship we had our first experience at eating in the mess hall standing up.

Luckily, this was a short trip and, the next morning when we were allowed on deck, we got our first look at Le Havre, France. It was a shock to say the least. In the water were hulls of some small boats still protruding where they had gone down. To one side was the twisted, broken and incongruous-looking remains of a bridge; to the other side was a mass of rubble with the frame-work of a house, or a chimney corner, the shell of a building still standing. It wasn't hard to believe the news reports of the fighting that had gone on there. But engineers and prisoners of war were already at work rebuilding.

Early that afternoon we were marched off the ship and on what we not-so-lovingly called a "forced march" of three miles to the train. It was in the heat of the day, we had on suits and overcoats we had slept in, we carried full packs; and if ever we were fed up with the Army it was that day for not providing transportation. The first impression the French people had of us could not have been good. We had a poor night's rest; we were hot and tired and angry, and we made only a half-hearted attempt to keep in order.

But eventually we did arrive at the station where, after waiting some time, we boarded a train of sorts. It was an old German train which had seen much better days. It had the compartments which appear to be standard in Europe; but also had holes on the top. Though there were openings for windows, there was no glass in them. Consequently—since of course it *had* to rain three or four times during the trip—we got uncomfortably wet. The utility coats we tried to hang over the window-openings did little good.

After we had waited in the train for perhaps three hours, and the French people in the station had all got a good look, the train did decide to pull out; but the trip seemed to consist of its running a few minutes and stopping, running and stopping. There was only one stop we really enjoyed—it was near a café where some colored soldiers spotted us and with loud yelps of surprise and joy, came running with bottles of wine and champagne, to the distinct annoyance of our officers.

That night, after the train had pulled up and stopped its allotted number of times, then backed up a good distance and at almost going-forward speed—onto another track, no doubt—we arrived at Rouen, France. Trucks were waiting and we were whisked away to our new quarters, which turned out to be one immense old building known as Caserne Tallandier and said to have once quartered Napoleon's troops, surrounded by several smaller ones and an eight-foot wall with a tall, iron gate.

All the enlisted women were assigned to the largest building, about thirty-two to a room. We still had double bunks, made of frames into which the Army cots had been fitted. For mattresses we were handed covers as we entered which we had to stuff with fresh straw from a pile outside. We found that when one lay down on it, it had a tendency to knot up, sticking one in the wrong places and sometimes biting. We had no sheets, no pillows; just blankets. Attempts had been made to fix up the building, however, and they continued throughout our stay. Showers had been provided (these ran all hot water, no cold); a laundry and ironing room had been fitted up. Prisoners of war were kept busy making ironing boards and clothes cabinets and such.

But little stumps a WAC. Those who felt they had to have pillows made them out of extra blankets, or coats, or robes. Those who couldn't bear the rough blankets scratching their necks (they weren't bound, you know, like our home blankets) found a piece of rag and folded it over the blanket edges. There was a broken pane in the window where my bunk-mate and I slept, and many were the nights we got rained or snowed on. I remember wrapping my head in my robe on several such occasions and going on back to sleep.

We had always felt more or less on display overseas. Now in Rouen we felt like monkeys in a cage, what with that wall and iron gate. For several days after our arrival, almost any time of day a host of French people and American soldiers could be found massed at the iron gate, looking in on us. Except for persons on business, visitors were not allowed inside until 7 p.m., and then only those with passes. At that hour every evening the soldiers poured in, and many were the happy meeting of old friends and husbands and sweethearts. I myself was elated to find my nephew, Lt. Thomas L. Pitts, stationed nearby. After he found me, he used to come over sometimes and take me out and, since enlisted women were not supposed to hobnob with officers, we had to get special permission to go out together. It was a novel experience to have to get special permission to go out with my own nephew! The French people, unable to come in, continued to stand at the gate and stare. When we were able to get passes and go outside, they would stop in the middle of the street or anywhere and openly gape at us.

We found Rouen much like Le Havre. Rubble everywhere, bits of buildings completely gutted, the very old and exquisitely carved cathedral nothing but a shell. Of course the entire city had not been leveled; but in spots it was a shambles. And I never looked at all the debris without thinking of the human beings who had gone down with it. We never saw actual warfare; but with what was around us, it was not too hard to imagine what it was like. America can thank God that that total war was not fought on home ground.

Still, Rouen had much of interest and we got our first taste of French life there. We saw the oldest clock in the world on one of Rouen's narrow little streets; we saw the spot where Joan of Arc was burned at the stake. We got our first sight of street cafés, and we learned to wrestle with the French language. I wasn't so good at the language business, but did learn a few halting words most Americans do and, supplementing with the universal sign-language, managed somehow.

After a time we were issued passes—some to Paris, some to Brussels. Mine was to Paris, in charge of ten other girls. And how can I adequately describe that famed City of Lights? Physically untouched by the war (the French Government had surrendered to Hitler, and Paris was not bombed), it could be viewed in all its glory, and we gloried in all it had to offer—Notre Dame Cathedral, the Sorbonne, the Place de la Concorde, the Seine River on one bridge of which stands the original Statue of Liberty, the Left Bank, the Eiffel Tower, the Palace of Marseilles with its priceless tapestries and paintings and Hall of Mirrors, the Champs Elysses, the Louvre Museum, the shops, the Metro, the gay and busy sidewalk cafés, the Follies Bergere.... The Red Cross Patio Club, where we stayed, was just around the corner from the Place Vendome, the Place de la Concorde, and the apartment where Chopin lived and died. Seeing these historic places, walking through the centuries, as it were, was to me an invaluable experience.

We caused a little flurry at the Patio Club. We were given excellent quarters, but, being the first Negro WACs to stay there, when we entered the dining room those in charge seemed flustered and didn't quite know what to do with us. (Red Cross clubs were largely segregated in those days, as were the Services.) They seated us the first time in a far-off corner together. After that we purposely ignored this seating and plopped down wherever we chose. We were not molested. We made it a point to appear, too, in the courtyard—a pleasant place where snacks were served and service-women were wont to relax in the afternoons.

In Paris, as elsewhere abroad, colored WACs were a surprise. White as well as Negro soldiers looked at us as if they couldn't believe their eyes. They'd yell anywhere, "American WACs!" and usually follow with the line: "You're the first American (or colored) girl I've seen in three (or two) years!" It was almost impossible for us to sit at a street café and pay for our own drinks; someone almost always invariably came along and insisted on treating.

Back in Rouen we suffered a great tragedy. Three of our girls—Mary Bankston, Mary Barlow and Delores Brown—went off one afternoon, with some others, for an outing at one of the men's camps. They never came back. The Army vehicle in which they were riding had an accident, killing two of them instantly; the third died a few days later. We were left completely stunned, and I know none of us will ever forget.

I will never forget, either, the accident my nephew had. Handsome and debonair, he had made a hit with my Company's female officers and often came over to visit them. Leaving our area one night, driving his own jeep, he had an accident which put him in the hospital and kept him there for some time. For a while, because of this, I was a privileged character on Post. My Commanding Officer put her car at my disposal so that I could visit the hospital, and once she accompanied me there. Tommy wasn't very glad to see us that time; his face was swollen and scarred, and he was ashamed. But he did get over his injuries and lived to frequent our area again.

In June of 1945 I requested discharge. I thought I had had enough of Army discipline and restrictions. (I was wrong, and later regretted my decision.) In July orders came through for me, and three others who had made such requests (Adele Ricketts, Eloise McNeely and Bernice Huggar), to proceed without delay to Compiegne, France, there to await transportation to the States. I had to hasten with my packing, being informed that "without delay" meant leaving in two days. The day before we were to leave I was surprised with a special dinner planned by my Company B Commanding Officer, Lt. Tonkins, attended also by Captain Kearney, our Executive Officer, and the entire Company B. I was pleasantly stunned that all this was for me, and the lump in my throat threatened to make me a bawling baby, especially when two of my pals sang for me two parting songs—"I'll Be Seeing You," and "We'll Meet Again." My cup ran over that day, for later even several *officers* invited me to their quarters for farewells and gifts!

Came Sunday morning and the four of us took final leave of our battalion, amid some tears and many envious good-byes. We returnees, as the four of us were called thereafter, proceeded to Compiegne and thence to Choicy Du Bac, where the WACs were quartered in that area. There we joined a number of white WACs also on their way home.

It was in the Compiegne Forest that France had signed its armistice with Germany in June of 1940 and, as shown in that often-seen news photograph, Hitler had performed his dance of joy. But since D-Day in June of 1944, Allied armies had been crushing the Germans of their sweep through France and had reached and liberated Paris in August of that year.

Choicy Du Bac was a group of tents set in the clearing of a forest of tall trees. From the road outside, the tents were completely hidden and only the mess hall and the chateau, which served as headquarters, were visible. It was a beautiful setting but a somewhat rugged life with dirt floors (we were always stumbling over tree roots), plain army cots and just blankets for bedding. Shower-baths were had upon occasion by the way of a portable contraption parked by the Seine River across the road; wash-ups meantime from the familiar old tin washbasin. The latrine, in another tent, was up the road and a bit inconvenient if you had to find it in the wee, very dark hours of the night. But if you could forget practical inconveniences such as these and concentrate on the setting—well, it was something. Something to lie on your cot and see how the sun fell through the branches of the trees; to listen to the soft patter of light rain on our tent-top; to stand back and observe the coloring of the trees—bronze, light green, almost red, dark green, yellow. . . . And really something, coming from the open-air movies about midnight, almost to feel, rather than see, the moonlight and starlight.

But I fear the setting did not receive the appreciation it might have under other circumstances. We had been hurried from our outfits, were anxious to get home, and were under the impression we would leave immediately by plane. But someone snafued the plans and at Choicy Du Bac we stayed nearly three weeks, making reveille and retreat and attending orientation classes on, of all things, life in the United States. It seemed so silly and time-wasting. If you don't learn patience in the Army you will *never* learn it. The idea always seems to be to rush you somewhere, and then have you wait and wait and wait for something to happen. This was no exception and there was considerable griping about it. To calm us down a bit, the powers came forth with a tour of Napoleon's lavish old castle at Pierrefonds, with its gorgeously decorated rooms and huge concrete slots through which, in the olden days, the castle inhabitants dropped great stones and burning oil down on intruders. Then some of us who wished it got five-day passes to Paris. I wished it, of course, and so got my second chance to see the fabled city. As it happened, some of the friends I had left in Rouen were there on pass when I arrived and, when we came upon each other, there were mutual cries of surprise and delight. Another second chance!

I teamed up with them, naturally, and we did have some wonderful times. There was, in particular, a little café on a side-street where we spend most of our evenings. It was cozy and attractive, filled always with a crowd of friendly people. There was a piano on a platform in the center, available for anyone to play, and one of our girls took over. It all lives in my memory as a warm and pleasant interlude.

We colored girls also spent some time acting as what we called a "voluntary USO unit." Soon after we arrived, a Negro soldier billeted nearby saw us, and before long every Negro soldier in the vicinity knew we were there. Most of them had been in combat and had recently come down from Germany. They followed the usual line, vowing we were the first colored women they had seen in from one to three years, and vied with each other in providing parties and special dinners for us at their camps. They seemed so elated at the sight of us and so eager to show their appreciation that we quite wore ourselves out, trying to let all of them see us and dance with us and do the things they wanted to do for us.

Eventually, after nearly three weeks, we were ordered to Le Havre where, we were told, we would embark within the next day or two. The forty-one of us piled on our trucks and were driven through Senlis, Chantilly (home of the famous lace), St. Denis, Pontoise and—again—Rouen, to Le Havre. At Le Havre we were quartered in a chateau literally perched on top of the world, at the ocean, where we stayed for considerably more than a day or two. But we lived rather well. We had four solid walls about us, latrines on the inside, and a real bath-tub. There were double bunks with mattresses and sheets (though still no pillows); and our meals were served at table by French waitresses.

Right on our grounds were filled-in fox holes and a huge pill-box built in the rocks. On the top of the pill-box still hung the rope nets with which soldiers not so long past had camouflaged their guns; and when we started to walk up a path behind it one day, a French girl called out that there were old mines that way. Before you could say "-b out face," we had done it and proceeded in another direction.

After a week at the chateau, we were ordered farther up the hill to Camp Home Run, and there for two nights we lived in Nissen huts and slept on straw mattresses again, so lumpy one had to have a back like a camel to fit into them.

Saturday, August 11, while were sitting in the movie, someone came in and yelled: "AT EASE! Japan surrendered at 1400 today!" Everyone jumped up, screamed, cried, kissed the person siting next, and joined the crowd milling out. The announcement, of course, was a bit premature; but we didn't know it then and got on with our celebration. (The surrender actually came on August 14, when we were at last on the high seas heading for home.)

That night of August 11 we were informed that we would embark on the *Thomas H. Barry*, a small liner, the next morning; so on Sunday morning, August 12, we finally began our journey home. The ship was overcrowded with us, more than 4300 white troops, USO workers and internees, but we didn't care. At least the WACs were considered first-class passengers and enjoyed such privileges as four-course meals in the officers' dining room, and a part of the deck, off-limits to the soldiers, where we could go and stay as long as we chose. Some of the WACs were asked to serve as disc-jockeys for records that were kept going, and I was one of those who served. Two or three days of the voyage were pretty rough and many a voyager was seasick (I wasn't this time either); but for the most part it was a real sentimental journey home.

Monday, August 20, amidst a loud and enthusiastic reception from the boats which came out to meet us, the *Barry* docked at Camp Shanks. Even to us, who had been away only six months, it was good to be home. The white girls, who had been away two and three years, were overjoyed. They exclaimed about everything just because it was American—houses, signs, streets, automobiles, the people to whom they did not have to ask "Parlez-vous Anglais?"

At Shanks we gorged ourselves on the steak dinner traditionally served returning soldiers and prepared to move on the next morning to separation centers. In the evening two of the white girls—one from Georgia, the other from Virginia—came to our rooms and said to us, "It's been a pleasure knowing you girls. We have learned something and you have certainly demanded our respect. We're proud of you."

To the four of us that meant a great deal. From the time we were ordered to Compiegne, we and thirty-seven white girls had been thrown closely together. Most of the white girls were from the South—Georgia, Virginia, Texas; and the First Sergeant was from Mississippi. For over a month we lived (though we slept in separate tents), bathed, ate, made formations and played together. They had undoubtedly never associated with Negroes before in their lives, and it was immensely gratifying to us to know we had given them the right first impression.

We were gratified by something else, too. It had been judged that our outfit, the 6888th Central Postal Directory, was "one of the best and most efficient WAC units in the entire WAC and had accomplished one of the greatest jobs of the war." We had the good feeling of a job well done and were proud to have been a part of the 6888th.

The next day we were broken into smaller groups and sent out in various directions. With nine others I went to Fort Sheridan, Illinois; two days later I was handed my Honorable Discharge plus the little old ruptured duck—the Veteran's Pin. And so ended, for me, the great WAC adventure.

Was it worth it? You bet it was. First off, it gave me a good feeling of having done my part in the war effort. In some Negro quarters today it is apparently suicide for your standing for a Negro to say he loves his country and will do what he can to defend it. No matter. This is my country—good, bad or indifferent, and the only one I know; so I feel I have the right and the responsibility to help preserve it—if not for altruistic reasons, then just to save my own hide.

I enjoyed the work, the new friends made, the camaraderie, the travels which allowed me at last to see some of the far-away places I'd been longing to see. I appreciated the opportunity to continue doing what I could toward the improvement of race relations both here and abroad and, as you have seen, the results were on the positive side.

There were other intangible gains: Learning to do without some basic necessities we always thought we could *not* do without; ingenuity, which means not only making do with what we had, but making it do more—

like improvising drapes out of GI towels, using lighter fuel to clean our un-washable clothes, holding up our oversize work pants with straps and cords from our musette and utility bags instead of with the belts we didn't have. We learned patience (hurry up and wait!) and endurance (we did not face the conditions the boys faced, but ours were certainly no bed of roses), and teamwork—the *esprit de corps* which was so effective and wonderful.

All the time, of course, there were things which could be criticized—inefficiency and blundering in some places, inequities, unnecessary hardships, some of our officers. There was the racial segregation.

But for me the good outweighed the bad and I do not for a moment regret that I was once a WAC.

Epilogue

I can't let the WAC comrades I left back in Rouen just drop out of the picture; so I must report that they remained in Rouen until September of 1945 when they moved to Paris. I am told that they lived at the Bohy Lafayette Hotel which was within walking distance of Sacre Coeur, the Place de L'Opera and the Follies Bergere, all of which provided them with plenty of opportunities for sightseeing and recreation after the day's work, and they did not fail to take advantage.

It was all over in February of 1946 because then all those left in the ranks (many had been discharged earlier) were returned to the States. Our great lady, Mary McLeod Bethune, was to greet them at the docks in New York when they arrived in early March but could not make it. She asked me to go in her place and of course I jumped at the chance. When I showed up on the platform where the girls were standing in formation awaiting further orders, and they finally recognized me in my civvies, we had a grand and glorious reunion.

The group broke up after that and the 6888th CPD ceased to be. Some of the girls were discharged; others chose to make the WAC a career and first went on leave, then some were assigned to Halloran Hospital on Staten Island, the others to Camp Stoneman in California, later to Camp Beale and then to Fort Ord. Still later, many went other places. My friend

Ruth Jacobs, for example, spent some years in Japan. She retired in 1964 after 20 years' service; my friend Novella Auls retired in 1967 after 25 years. They and many others were still in to see the great change from segregation to integration and the change of the WAC "duration" designation as a part of the AUS—Army of the United States—to the permanent designation as a part of the USA—United States Army.

I am still in touch with some with whom I served and have met many others since my return to civilian life. Many I have unfortunately lost track of. But the bond between WACs is strong, whether in touch or out of touch and I, for one, will remember and hold dear all of them. They became an important part of my life when we shared the great WAC adventure.

Lucia Pitts's graduation photo, New Trier Township High School, Winnetka, Illinois, June 1920.

Lucia Pitts's home church, Pilgrim Baptist Church, Chicago, June 1964. Photographer Harold Allen. (Courtesy of Library of Congress Prints and Photographs Division, Washington, DC)

Ten enlisted WACs leaving Fort Huachuca, Arizona, for overseas training. *Front row, left to right:* PFC Dorothy Louise Reid; T5 Lucia M. Pitts; PFC Marie Gillisslee; PVT Charlotte Cartwright; T5 Edna Burton. *Back row, left to right:* Lt. Consuelo Bland, commanding officer; T4 Evelyn Martin; PVT Mildred Peterson; T5 Alice Allison; T5 Fannie Talbert; PFC Mildred Gates. (*Indianapolis Recorder,* January 20, 1945, Sec. 2, p. 1, Hoosier State Chronicles, Indiana State Library)

Lucia Pitts's WAC friends (*clockwise from top left*) Novella Auls, Jerrel (Jerry) Lawrence, Delores B. Mariano, and Malinda Ann Washington. (Courtesy of the National Afro-American Museum and Cultural Center, Novella Auls Collection)

To celebrate V-E Day, the 6888th Battalion B Company commander, First Lt. Vashti B. Tonkins of Virginia, leads the company in a parade at the marketplace in Rouen, France, where Joan of Arc had been executed. In the second row are Second Lt. Alice Eizabeth Edwards, First Lt. Blanche Leona Scott, and First Lt. Willia Gene Cherry. May 27, 1945. (Courtesy of National Archives, RG111, SC426441)

Company B marches past the equestrian statue of Napoleon Bonaparte. Rouen, France, June 1945. (Courtesy of the Portsmouth Athenaeum, Doris Moore WWII Album)

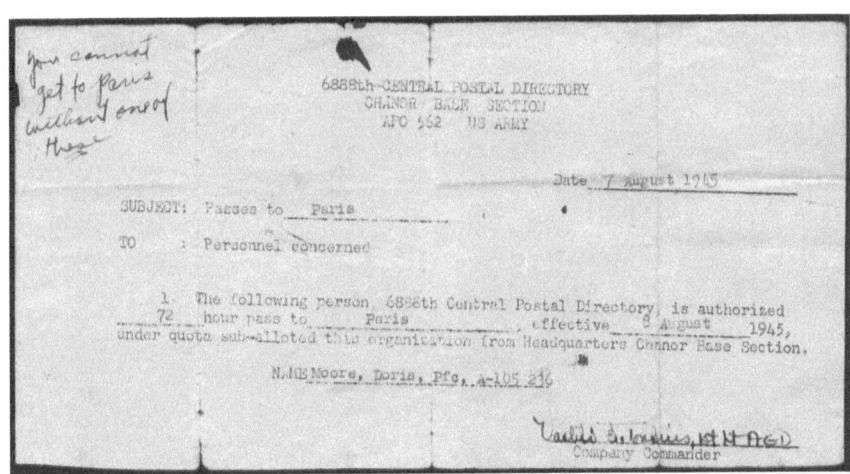

A travel pass to Paris, signed by Lucia Pitts's company commander, First Lt. Vashti B. Tonkins, August 7, 1945. (Courtesy of the Portsmouth Athenaeum, Doris Moore WWII Album)

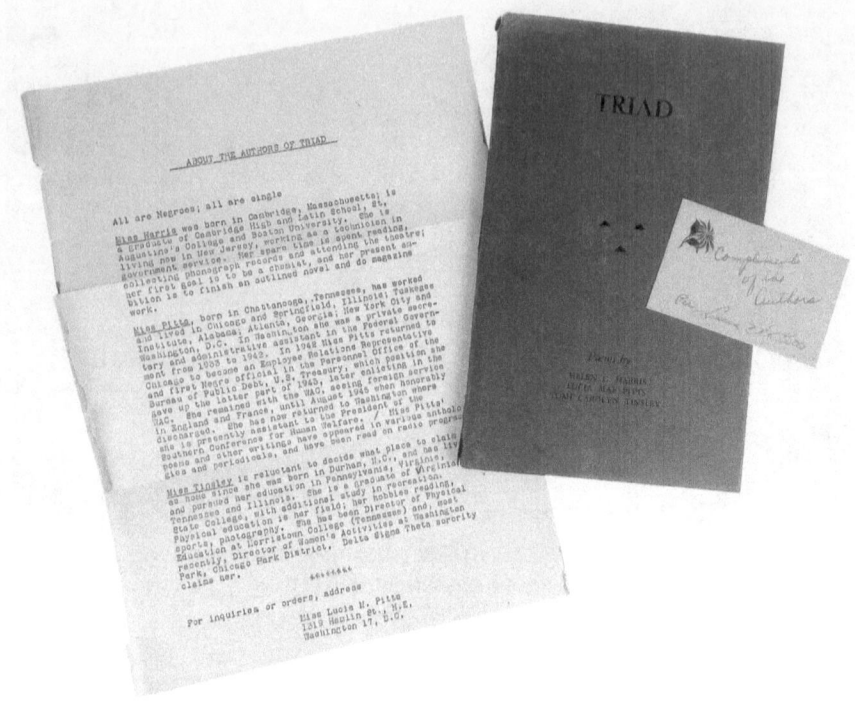

Lucia Pitts's book, *Triad,* and a letter about the book, December 1945

Private Lucia Pitts at work, Fort Huachuca, Arizona. (*Apache Sentinel,* April 7, 1944, 7)

Selected Poems

This section includes one hundred of Lucia Pitts's best poems, arranged thematically, beginning with poems on War and the Military. With the exception of "Farewell," which concludes the War and the Military section, the poems appear chronologically within their respective thematic groupings: Nature, Love and Romance, Friendship, The Circle of Life, Art, and Punctuation Suite.

War and the Military

The following poems are inspired by Lucia Pitts's experiences with the US Army during World II. They reflect her firsthand experience as an African American woman soldier.

Brown Moon

Dedicated to the 99th Pursuit Squadron, Tuskegee Institute, Alabama

Bright moon
Up yonder in God's skies
Radiant brown, you moon;
For I am brown,
Through eyes of brown

I see you,
And brown is
A soothing, enchanting
Color.

Brown moon,
Up there in the skies,
Look out on our boys
Wherever they be.
Somewhere out there
They are riding the air—
Our brown flyer boys.

Brown moon,
Guide them right;
Be their searchlight.
For in your care
Are they—
Our brown flyer boys
Somewhere
Out there....

Dear moon,
Down here
The seasons will move unerringly in—
The lush and vivid autumn days,
The winter—fierce and cold and white;
Spring and summer, with trees blossoming
And the red, red roses
Swaying in the breeze—
The night breeze over the gardens,
Gentle and kind.

But oh, my moon
Out there our boys will be riding,

Piercing the air.
For them no sweet-smelling buds
Nor quiet breezes playing
In the moonlight
Over the tranquil gardens
Of home.
The darkness of night for them,
And, blinding their eyes,
A passionate anger
Against the stalking mob
Which comes to assault our homes
And break our peace.
They may lose the way
And be forever lost
Without God's soft clouds
And you.

So moon, silver-brown moon.
With trembling lips
And torn heart,
On the symphony of the winds
I breathe my prayer—

Light the way
For our boys
Riding the air
Out there. . . .

Opportunity (November 1942): 336; *Bitter Fruit: African American Women in World War II* (1999): 267–68.

A WAC Speaks to a Soldier

"Editor's Note: The following poem is used in commemoration of the week of May 11 to May 18, which has been officially designated by the War Department as 'WAC Week.' Pfc. Pitts designates it to her nephew, Lt. Thomas L. Pitts, now stationed somewhere in England with a quartermaster outfit, to soldiers at Fort Huachuca and to all soldiers in order that they may better appreciate what the Women's Army Corps stands for."—*Apache Sentinel*

We salute you—
But not with so common a thing as our hands.
Our hands must keep busy working
And we cannot keep them raised
For as long as you need saluting.
It is our hearts that we raise as a gesture of respect—
Quietly and unseen.
But constantly and reverently.

You did not really want us here.
"Women have no place in the Army," you said.
"Women should stay at home and keep the home-fires burning.
We want to think of you as sitting and waiting
For us to come back,
Dressed in the flimsy gowns which were yours alone
And which we remember sentimentally;
Not in a uniform like thousands and thousands of others
And so much like our own.
We want to dream of you
As lying down to your rest at night,
Looking up at the stars and the moon above us all
And saying a prayer for us."
Others said, "You were cruel to come in
And push us out to the firing line . . .
Do you know you are sending us out to our death?"

We have swallowed your disapproval
And joined up just the same,
Because there was a job to be done
And we had to do it.
We have tried not to think of things
Like sending you to your death.
We have thought, on the other hand,
Of what would happen to all of us
If you stayed at home . . .

We have come in to share as much as we can
Of your discomfort and your sacrifice.
We, too, march, and soil ourselves with dirty jobs
And rise with the dawn to put in a good day's work
At the jobs you did before.
When we seek our bunks at night,
Our bodies, too, are weary and sore.
And as we take over and push you from your jobs over here,
We salute you.
With a lump in our throats and determination in our hearts,
We salute you.

We come to do you and our country good.
We believe in you.
We believe it will not be in vain.
You will go forth as men of whom we may be proud,
For whom we shall be glad to have left
The comfort of our homes,
The security of our paying jobs,
The freedom of action we knew—
For whom we shall be glad to have shared
The sacrifice you make.
We will not let you down.
Though not in the delicate gowns you knew,

Though not sitting, but still waiting,
We shall keep the home-fires burning.
And from the austerity of our Army home,
We will seek the stars and the moon
And say our prayers ...

We send you forth,
And as you go marching in never-ending files,
With our hearts and the work of our hands
We salute you.

Apache Sentinel (May 19, 1944): 1, 8; *Bitter Fruit: African American Women in World War II* (1999): 40–41.

Let Them Come to Us

Now they go forth to war,
Our white brothers across the sea,
Speaking wistfully of peace.
They have known peace;
Now they go forth to war.

We who are black,
All the days of our lives
We have known war;
All the days of our years
We have lived war.
We are not acquainted with peace;
But if our brothers would learn of war,
Let them come to us.

If they would know aggressors
Let them come to us and hear how we, forever long,
Have been sat upon by demons of hate

That spring from hearts that know us not
But attack us still.
Hear how, not for one or five years of our lives
But for eighty long years and two,
We have been made to defend ourselves
Against the unseen and the seen, within and without—
    inertia and indifference, violence and hate,
    starvation and sickness, envy and betrayal,
    ignorance and illiteracy, guns and bombs,
    misunderstanding and injustice,
    ropes and faggots . . .
Hear how these aggressors and countless more
Have invaded our homes and left them a shambles,
Robbed our hearths of fathers and sons,
Laid waste our growing fields,
Hanged our hearts on the tree . . .

If they would know aggressors,
Let them come to us.
If they would face the foe unflinching,
If they would learn to fight unceasing,
Let them come to us and see—
See how, with unflagging hearts and heads and hands,
Out of the dust that sifted under our nomadic feet
And the blood of our fathers spilled in battle,
We have fashioned men.
See how, with too little for food,
We have made them strong—
Strong to run, strong to fight,
Strong to dig the world's ditches,
Lay its gleaming rails across the land
And push its buildings up to brush the skies.
See how, by candle-light and guttering lamps,
And by the kindly light of the moon

We have taught our men and made them wise,
So that now they walk serene and unfaltering
With men of tools and plows and figures,
Men of medicine and law and government,
Those of frocks and words and palettes,
The world of footlights and music and song . . .

Then let them look again and see
How we, grown strong and wise,
Have trampled the mountains and the plains,
The long and thickly matted swamps,
Sodden with the blood of our neighbors,
Our fathers and our brothers,
To meet the foe and face him down—
How we have faced both master and menial
In open combat and in hidden dug-out,
And snipers in the world's labyrinth passes.
We have faced unafraid the marching invader;
We have met death by cruel violence
At the hands of "persons unknown."
But in spite of the numberless wounded and dead,
We have plunged on and never turned back.

If they would know the strength to fight,
Let them come to us.
If they would have faith—
If they would keep hope forever alive,
If they would know patience akin to Job's,
Let them come to us and learn
The faith of our fathers;
Behold the hope that, dying, is reborn
And lives again to stiffen up our backs;
See with what patience we have borne
The pain and the losses of all these years.

If they would know hope and faith and patience,
Let them come to us.

If they would know victory in the end,
Our white brothers who go to war,
Let them come and walk with us
Who push forever on,
Who have fought a thousand wars
And died a thousand deaths,
Yet snatched victory from defeat.

Now they go forth to war,
Speaking wistfully of peace.
We, who are black, have known no peace,
But if our brothers would learn of war,
Let them come to us.

1940
Honorable Mention
National Negro Exposition

Triad (1945): 117–20; *Ebony Rhythm* (1948): 46–48.

This Is the Thing We Ask

Is it worth it?
This leaving, I mean, to travel
On the face of this dark earth
To places out of reach of comforting arms—
In durance to live and fight and pray,
To toil in blood, to fence with death—
Or but through long monotonous hours
To push the pen across the page,
To tap the clacking keys—
To part with limb and sight and sound:

Is it worth it?
Will the reward we reap
In a finer, more tolerant world,
Make it up to us for all we've sacrificed
Through these endless, lonely days
When we walked and fought and died alone
In strange and unfamiliar places?
Will we bring back to you we left at home—
In fuller hearts, in richer minds,
In renewed faith and understanding—
Enough to compensate
For the anxious days we made you bear?
Will you have compassion and patience, and wait—
Will you wait, though the time be long?
Or when we come back again
Will we find you have forgot
And turned, and walked another way from ours?

Through the hours empty of all but urgent thought,
This is the thing I ask myself—
These are the things we ask,
A million of us and more.
For the hours are empty,
Though only to ourselves do we confess.
The days must be got through somehow,
And one must smile, be brave and gay,
Toss careless banter back and forth,
Hobnob with first this one, then that,
And go about our ordered, grim tasks
With calm and fortitude—
Though the heart lies heavy deep inside.

Was it for this we came?
When annihilation is over and done,

When the bloody fields are green again
And peace has stayed the hand of reaching Death,
What then—what then?

This is the thing we ask.

ENGLAND
1945

Triad (1945): 39–40.

Franklin Delano Roosevelt

It is not ours to say
How history will record you.
Justice is not always done
On this earth.
We do not know what you were like
When you closed the shades
On the gaping populace.
We cannot swear to what was in
Your so-strong heart,
What reasons lay back in your eager mind
When you did some things
The people thought should not have been done,
Or did not do the things we thought
You should have done.

Yet to us you were a great man.
You were a brave and gallant man
Who went down to death fighting
That other men might be free—
Who gave his life to the cause
For which Christ long ago gave His:
The cause of justice, and mercy, and peace.

You were a Moses
Who went into the far reaches of his domain
And bade men set my people free...

These are poor words, and trite.
These are small words
For a great man.
But let them be our way to say
God rest you.
God grant you lasting peace and reward.
Justice *is* done in that realm
To which you go.

ENGLAND

Triad (1945): 35.

Little Café

There's a little café on a Paris side-
street, etched deep in my memory...
It's a picture I never will forget—
that my heart forever will see...
Champagne was on the table and a piano
sat near-by... The setting was so per-
fect, I wanted foolishly to cry...
The mirror hanging on the wall, the
camaraderie, the people gay; the half-
moon seat we all sat on; the bar across
the way... All these are a part of the
picture etched deep in my memory; but
the music was the center of it, and
even now I see the figure at the piano,
and hear the songs we sang... I see slim
fingers on the keys; recall how my heart

rang . . . So that little café on a Paris
side-street is etched deep in my memory . . .
a picture I never will forget, and a
picture only for me . . .

PARIS
JULY 1945

Triad (1945): 54.

Farewell

Out of the stillness three lonely shots,
Clear and solemn . . .
Taps . . .
To those who gave their utmost,
Farewell, farewell,
Farewell!

Chicago Defender (November 14, 1931): 15.

Nature

The beauty and optimism of nature, especially that of flowers, clouds, trees, and water, are recurring tropes in Pitts's verse.

To My Flowers

Like a crown at the end of a perfect day,
Like a beautiful thought that no words can portray,
    Are my flowers.
And the cares of the day that have gone before.
The aches and the pains, and the hurts evermore

    Are lost in my flowers.
My weary soul rests, and my spirit grows calm
In the fragrance and beauty—the sheer, cooling balm
    Of these, my flowers.
For these little blossoms with the healing of God.
Thanks be to Him, and for the seed, rain and sod
    That made my flowers.

Chicago Defender (April 18, 1925): A12.

Fallen Castles

There was a morn—soft and cool, it was—
    When I stood on a wind-swept hill
And stretched my body in the joy of life.
    And listened to a tinkling rill.

There was a noon—bright and warm, that day—
    When I thrilled in the work at my hands;
When hope was high and faith was strong,
    And I believed in my fair plans.

There came the eve—gray and soft blue—
    When beauty seemed everywhere:
When even the most forlorn of life
    Seemed imbued with beauty rare.

And then the night—with a moon overhead,
    Dripping silver tears below:
The sound of waters under a breeze's command,
    And the smell of good things that grow.

But life is so cold, and dreams are so short—
    My beautiful day has long fled.

And here stand I, unclothed, uncertain;
    But a crown of pain on my head.

On low ground I stand. Where does life take our faith?
    Why our heart-made hopes so destroy?
Oh, answer there must be—for answer I cry!
    Are we just so many small toys?

Gone are my dreams—only facts may I see—
    Unyielding, unkind and unfair.
Desolate my heart—oh, God, must this be?
    Send back dreams to one in despair!

Chicago Defender (November 21, 1925): A10.

A Lonely Soul

A lonely soul
Lay in a sordid room
With nothing in life to live for.
The room was bare,
The soul was warped
And the heart was broken and sore.

But a tiny bird
Thru a broken pane
Flew in and sang and sang
Till the room seemed filled
With beautiful light
And the rafters with music rang.

So the soul was lifted,
The heart was mended,
And, after all, life held a bit of song.

Dear precious bird
From the hand of God,
There's a world waiting for you to come along!

Chicago Defender (July 30, 1927): A2.

Clouds

The clouds,
Like banks of clean, creamy snow,
Are piled against the sky
In silver groups
As if apart
From the background
Of clear, quiet blue.
Westward,
Over a distant hilltop,
The dipping sun
Points through an armful
Of these clouds,
Suffusing them with a rosy flush;
These then separate,
Grouping together here and there
Until I think I can see
A hidden city
Back of them.
With the spear-points
Of the sun,
Like glowing spires,
Leaping upward,
With dreamy castles
Thrusting themselves
Heavenward.
And glory a-gleam

Everywhere. . . .
Here is the city of Heaven
Indeed—
In the clean, creamy
Clouds. . . .

      THE LADY CALLED LOU.
      (AT TUSKEGEE)

Chicago Defender (October 29, 1927): A2.

Sky Dreams

Oh, I'd like a fine white galloping steed
 To ride across the sky,
With the heavenly blue all about me there
 And the wind a-flying by!

I'd like to touch those fluffy clouds
 And pillow them 'bout my face;
Then if a comet passed me by,
 On my white steed give chase.

I'd like to see how gold the clouds get
 When the sun goes down at day's end;
And if I got cold, I'd warm myself
 By the fire the sun would send.

Oh, I'd like to be in those glorious tints,
 When the sun goes down to rest,
That suffuse the sky below on high
 And halo the mountain's crest.

Oh, I'd like a fine white galloping steed
 To ride up in the sky,

When the moon comes out and the stars all about,
    And the wind a-flying by!

Chicago Defender (February 11, 1928): A2.

Daisies

I always wondered why it was
    That daisies wouldn't tell,
And now I know it's just because
    They've learned a lesson well.
A lady says they once were folks
    And, oh, how they did talk!
Till God got tired of their foolishness
    And hung 'em on a stalk.

I guess he closed their mouths an said
    "Now you can think all you dare
But not a word can you say about folks
    And from necessity, you'll take care."
So daisies now just smile all day—
    No matter what folks do,
They can't say a word about things that are so
    Or make up things that aren't true.

Say, doesn't it seem to you sometimes
    A lot of us would look swell
Swaying on a stalk in somebody's yard
    Where we could never tell?

Chicago Defender (March 10, 1928): A2.

Day of Rain

God!—the steady downpour
Beating on the earth.
Spattering on the Window-sill!
Fair-day paths running streams.
Tall trees—weeping giants,
Weeping with my heart.
Rain—long, long day of rain!

A veil of darkness
Shut off the sky
And God Himself couldn't see
The earth.
So He made a point of light
Swiftly darting through the dark;
Then reached out His hand
To bring in the light.
And so powerful was He
That the breeze from the moving
Of His hand
Reverberated through all the land.
Crashed against the dripping of the rain
And shattered the silence apart,
Lightning—thunder!

God . . . the steady downpour
Flowing from the roof.
Spattering on the sill . . .
Great trees—weeping giants,
Weeping with my heart.
Rain—long, long day of rain!

Chicago Defender (June 23, 1928): A2; *Washington Tribune* (May 4, 1935): 6.

And We, We Fain Would Leave It All Behind

Well, folks, I've worshipped now at the shrine of Booker T. Washington since last September. I've roasted in Tuskegee Institute's heat and reveled in its yearning nights when the stars hang low; I've praised its mild winter days and gloried in its marvelously beautiful and entrancingly green spring days. I've seen the bluest sky and the whitest clouds in the world and I've feasted my eyes on the most gorgeous sunsets of East or West, North or South. I've worked like a Trojan, and perhaps I've made a friend or two.

Yet, in spite of it all, I dream of the streets of Chicago, the skyscrapers brushing lips against the clouds, the lake the hustle and bustle of the place, the people and—oh, all about it, disillusioning, searing and heartless as it sometimes is. So now I turn my footsteps northward for a day or a month—or who knows how long?—hoping that here at Tuskegee I've learned a little, accomplished a little and done a little good. July 1st will hear me saying—Chicago, here I am!

Chicago Defender (July 7, 1928): A2.

Forest at Dusk

Slender, straight pines
Standing still
Against the deepening darkness,
Clinging close together
As they climb
Toward heaven:
A disclike moon
Ogling through
Out of a dusky sky.
A tingling, piney odor
And hushed quiet.
Out of the silence,

A drowsy bird
In the shadows
Chirping to its mate—
Humming time!
Tall, slender pines
Standing straight
Against a dusky sky.

Chicago Defender (January 26, 1929): A2.

City Streets on a Rainy Day

City streets on a rainy day—
Rivers of water lining the way.
Oh, I know how black your pavements are
Rainy days and dark, with no gleaming star
To light the way, as sometimes at night
Guides straying, weary footsteps aright.

I've walked the streets in the piercing cold
When God seemed far and hope seemed old:
I've trudged the walks in the deathly heat—
Fire burning through thin shoes to my feet.
From the streets, in vain, I've searched for my star—
(Oh, I know how cruel your pavements are!)

Yet surely there must be times they are gay—
When worries and fears are all fled away.
But I remember best when I walked them in pain—
In the piercing cold and the stinging rain.
Pockets penniless—soul and body at war.
Oh, streets, how bleak your pavements are!

Chicago Defender (November 9, 1929): A2; reproduced and revised in *Chicago Defender* (July 18, 1931): 13.

Dream of Lavation

It seems an age I've dreamed of these
Of sailing on the moonlit seas,
Of traveling over foreign lands
Where romance still pervades and stands
With out-stretched arms to comfort souls
Grown weary with the search for goals.
It seems I've dreamed of how, for years,
Soft lapping water in my ears,
Moon like quicksilver on each wave,
This calm and quiet would gently lave
My smarting wounds and give me peace.
Then should I have happy release
From all the cares that bend men low.
I have but dreamed a dream. I know. . . .!

Afro-American (Baltimore, MD) (October 14, 1933): 18.

Afternoon Off

My poor wealth had been spent, that afternoon off,
And my purse was distressingly flat.
There was really no accounting for it, at all—
It had simply gone. Just like that.

I chided myself as I threaded my way
Down New Street, in and among the crowd.
Oh, I said quite awful things to myself.
And I *would* do better, I vowed.

But then I saw them—the flower vendors, I mean,
With blossoms of every bright hue.

And—well, five shillings went for the yellow ones.
Don't chide . . . Food for my soul was overdue.

ENGLAND
APRIL 1945

Triad (1945): 49; *Ebony Rhythm* (1948): 121–22.

Love and Romance

Throughout her career, Lucia Pitts wrote love poems depicting independent women, untrammeled by conventional, gendered roles. The journalist and poet Frank Marshall Davis felt that these strikingly frank and honest love poems, informed by modernist innovation as well as the blues, placed Pitts in the highest echelon of American poets. He observed, "Lucia Mae Pitts in her creations bears out our opinion that she consistently writes the best love poetry produced among our women."

To an Admirer

You come
Asking entrance to my heart;
You come with your clean manhood,
Rare in the world of today,
Knocking—seeking to touch me.
Ah, I am young—but old!
And men have made of my heart
A stone—hard and unyielding.
Yet you come with your great courage.
Knowing this, and understanding.
Boy, oh, my boy—for you,
May God let the doors of my heart
Swing open!

Chicago Defender (April 25, 1925): A10.

I Shall Come to Thee

Thy voice is my law and my joy—
It is no small thing with which to toy—
Ah, no: For when it comes my heart thrills
And quivers, till thou sayest to it—"Be still."
And when thou callest, where'er thou art,
Thy call shall come and reach my heart.
And I shall come to thee.

Thy voice is my law and a loved one.
The peace it brings is never done.
From the portals of heaven thou mayest call:
From the sands of the desert and their deathly pall;
Whene'er, where'er thou callest, thy voice I know well.
And tho thou callest from the depths of hell—
I shall come to thee.

Chicago Defender (July 4, 1925): A10.

All That I Ask

All that I ask of you, Dear Heart,
    Is that you love me long.
All that I ask of you to do
    Is listen to my song.
Merchants sell much that you may buy—
    All this I know is true.
But just your love, which can't be bought,
    Is all I ask of you.

The world has much to offer us
    Of pleasure, freedom, gold.
You, too, have much to offer one,

E'en while your heart is cold.
If hearts warm not, keep all these things—
    The things I want are few.
For just your love and faith, Dear Heart,
    Are all I ask of you.

Chicago Defender (August 8, 1925): A10.

A Flash

A blinding flash
In a whirling storm
Showed me the heavens' blue;
So a sudden word
In a world of pain
Showed me the heart of you.

A parched throat
On a desert vast;
How could I go on with no water near?
An aching heart
In an empty world;
How can I go on without you, dear?

Chicago Defender (July 16, 1927): A2.

Lines to a Certain Street

There's a certain charm you bear,
Old street.
It's not because you're fine
Or very neat,
Nor yet because your beauty
Is passing fair,

But because one whom I love truly
Once lived there.

Chicago Defender (August 13, 1927): A2.

That Which Endures

Seek to efface me from your precious sight,
Throw me out from your heart, if you will;
Break my body in half, as you have my heart,
And I shall love you still.

Let me do all things perchance to forget;
Let bitter words rain from my quill—
All in vain—forgive—oh, can't you see?
It's because I love you still!

Chicago Defender (August 27, 1927): A2.

If

If I should sigh for you tonight
And you should hear that call,
I wonder if you'd come to me,
Or would you care at all?

If I should want you very much
And of it you should hear,
I wonder if you'd laugh at me
Or come and kiss me, dear?

If I should pass away tonight
And you should learn of it,
I wonder if you'd care a little
And sorrow just a bit.

Oh, I shall never, never know
In life now or in death,
But when I'm gone, if you bend near
I shall feel your warm, sweet breath.

Chicago Defender (September 10, 1927): A2.

Brief Song

Here's to the road—the open road—
    And the dash of wind in my face;
A myriad of stars in the black above,
    And a moon set high up in space.

A long, long stretch of open road—
    A car that cuts the wind in two;
A humming motor that sings you to sleep,
    And you—you—you!

THE LADY CALLED LOU.
TUSKEGEE, ALA.

Chicago Defender (October 15, 1927): A2.

Song

OH, I'LL GO A'SINGING, SINGING, SINGING SONGS OF THE BENDING BLUE.

I know a tale on never a tongue—
I know a song that will never be sung;
In my heart it lies locked away
And I'll go singing other songs all day!

Oh, I'll go a-singing of the blue of the sky
And the stars and the moon hanging up high;

Oh, I will sing of the fairness of earth—
Songs full of gladness and songs full of mirth.

But there'll be one tale on never a tongue—
I'll have one song that will never be sung.
It's a song I'll never let go free—
The wonderful song you taught to me!

OH, I'LL GO A'SINGING, SINGING, SINGING SONGS OF THE BENDING BLUE.
AND NO ONE WILL KNOW HOW MY HEART GOES WINGING—WINGING
BACK TO YOU!

THE LADY CALLED LOU.
TUSKEGEE INSTITUTE, ALABAMA.

Chicago Defender (November 12, 1927): A2.

And Yet

They parted in anger—
No hint of hearts broken;
And yet—
Something akin to love
Oft sends a token.

Of murmuring memories
Flowing through the days.
And yet—
They ask of each nothing
As they seek out their ways.

Who can say if love's there—
If their hearts have spoken?
And yet—

Something warmly remembering
Oft sends a token.

Chicago Defender (February 4, 1928): A2.

Melody

So many desires form a part of our lives—
Many are the trinkets for which man strives.
Many are the dreams he builds to the skies,
Some of them hopeless and some of them wise.

What are the things I want most of all?
Forests of pines standing cool and tall;
Corn fields weaving and the wind singing through—
The caressing wind a-singing of you.

Sunsets flaming at the close of the day;
Dusk creeping quietly a-long the way.
Moonlight and starlight after sky's blue,
And a song in the darkness calling for you.

The husky cadence of your singing voice,
The melody calling my heart to rejoice;
A mem'ry of you, where'er you may be,
And the magical knowledge that you think of me.

Man's desires are blown down the years
Woven of joys, disappointment and tears,
But because I go finding you everywhere,
My heart has in it no place for despair—
The melody of you forever sings there!

Chicago Defender (February 18, 1928): A2.

Ways

You were born for faithlessness
And I for faith.

Perhaps in your own way
I am something to you—
And perhaps I am but a wraith—
Just a dream in blue.

So we will go our separate ways
Through starlit nights and wringing days.

I ask but that the wistful winds,
That breathe o'er lakes and fields of corn,
Blow back this message to your heart—
For faithfulness, dear, I was born.

Chicago Defender (March 31, 1928): A2.

Answering the Bubbles

I'm blowing bubbles in the air—
    Dreaming of things that should be;
I'm turning up my nose at care—
    I have to keep singing, you see.

I sing to a fanciful, mythical "you"—
    I doubt he could ever be.
And I sing of dreams grown up in my heart—
    Lost dreams—the soul of me.

So my "mystical" you is a "mythical" you
    Too ideal for things commonplace.

I think no man could ever be
    All my fancy may trace.

He lives perhaps—I do not know—
    My Ideals soar so high,
I'm merely blowing my bubbles up
    Feigning love, while life passes by.

Chicago Defender (April 7, 1928): A2.

Confession

TO THE REAL LOVE

I will not say I've been actually true—
    Of course, I've played around;
I will not even say I will ever be so,
    For loneliness has to be drowned.

Loneliness is like a shroud to me—
    A shroud in dreary black;
I can only suffer that weary gown
    When death lays my body back.

But love is like a glowing fire—
    Warm and cozy when burning.
Yet it cannot live without constant fuel—
    Oh, yes, you ace, I've been learning!

So, I must confess there've been other loves—
    But not even to them have I been true.
For all the while my heart's real love
    Was burning through to you!

Chicago Defender (June 9, 1928): A2.

Imagery

Oh, I could go the long way
    Forgetting life and time—
And I could go the strong way,
    Down roads gay and sublime—
I could go the long way—with you!

I could forget convention—
    The things that hold me tight;
Oh, I could break this tension
    That keeps me from the light!
I could forget conventions, with you.

Oh, I could give my life for love—
    Give it without thought;
Oh, I could endure strife with love
    And worlds with danger fraught.
I could give my life for love—of you.

Yet, I don't know where you are
    Nor even yet your name.
It does not matter—when you come
    I'll know the vehement flame.
And I will go the long way—with you!

Chicago Defender (June 16, 1928): A2.

I Was Thinking of You

He drove me down a ribbon of road—
    A road that met the blue:
He thinking of my comfort—of me—
    But I? I was thinking of you.

He sang to me sweet songs of love—
    Of loneliness and of rue.
We sang together, he and I,
    But I—I was singing of you.

He showed me where a rivulet ran—
    Where the loveliest flowers grew;
He dreamed of moonlight, me in his arms,
    But I? I was dreaming of you.

In the silver starlight, at road's end,
    He asked me to be true.
I could not answer—I pitied him—
    For I—I was thinking of you.

Chicago Defender (October 6, 1928): A2.

Beloved

Is it any wonder that I call it a dream—
This vision of you that is mine,
    My beloved?
Out of the maze of the years now past,
Into the present you forged your way.
In my heart now is your star's gleam;
Into my life pours ecstasy like wine,
    Darling, my beloved.

I have done little good to deserve all this;
Because I am undeserving I am humble bowed,
    My beloved.
But here you are, in my life, somehow—
Because the gods are good—are good!
There's nothing in life any more I can miss,

For everything worthwhile you've allowed,
    Darling, my beloved.

Ranting and raving—vain words mean nothing;
The stars were not there for us till they shown;
    So, beloved,
Beneath those stars that live their lights,
I pledge to show the things I say.
Whatever the years ahead, the fates may bring,
Our life will be like a rose full-blown,
    Darling, my beloved!

Chicago Defender (December 1, 1928): A2.

So You Have Come Back Again

So you have come back again
And I am here still with this pain—
This wild aching for you that for a space
Slept and I thought was dead—in its place
Sweet peace—no want of you.
But you have come back. What can I do?
Isn't it enough that my heart is yours?
Must you play with it so? Still, if it procures
For you any sort of pleasure, then you must
Have it your way. I cannot resist until dust
Has claimed my weary frame; and even then
I shall be yours if you come back again.

Chicago Defender (January 19, 1929): A2.

Daring Me to Forget

Yes, you have pained me—
Over and over again

Have you pained me.
But what is pain to me?
I have felt its sting before.
The pain has left its mark—
Where you have crucified me
Time and time again
There are scars—
Scars that in the black of night
I touch tenderly—
Because you made them.
For what else mean scars to me?
I have been bruised before.
So I do not hesitate to say
That I dream of you with longing
Still—
For the pain and the scars
Are but reminders of you
Daring me to forget.

Chicago Defender (January 19, 1929): A2.

Isn't It Strange?

I have put you firmly behind me.
Things of you belong to the past—
The ever receding past.
New things—other and lovelier people
Have filled your place
Quite wonderfully
And no more do you haunt me
As once you did.

But—isn't it strange
How ever so rarely.
A thought of you should intrude itself

Upon me
With such vivid force
And curious effect?
Isn't it strange?

Chicago Defender (February 2, 1929): A2.

I Went Back Over Old Things

Today I went back
Over old books—
Old poems that you had marked
And once we talked of
Together—
I went back
Over old things
With your touch on them—
I breathed the breath of you
In them still;
I inhaled the fragrance
Of your finger tips
That lingered where your fingers
Had lain.
My eyes tarried over foot notes
Once you had written.
And dim with tears, closed themselves
Something in me cried out
For a word of you again—
To have you send me things
You knew I'd like—
Because you liked them—
To read poems underlined by you.

Yes, I know—
Long ago you and I

Gave up our friendship.
Still, today I went back
Over old things with your touch
On them
And something in me
Cried out!

Chicago Defender (February 23, 1929): A2.

I'll Sing My Songs

It is a truth, the sages say,
That sorrow has its part to play
In this game that we call life.
They tell me when our days are rife
With tears (Oh, what a sorrowful thing!)—
Only then we are inspired to sing.

They say joy's but a common thing,
And common is the song we'll sing.
But the song of tears is the soul's song;
And so, they say, he does no wrong
Who gives one tears through which to sing—
To rise from earth on magic wing;
But my heart feels no want of tears—
Of stinging pain that wounds and scars.

Yet—the sages say this I must bear.
Ah, well—I'll pretend that I don't care.
Because of a pain which will never leave,
I'll sing my songs—thus shall grieve.

Chicago Defender (March 9, 1929): 14.

La Callada Voz

Out of the cold
A voice—
Out of the silence
A sound;
And wherever birds fly against
The sky,
Vagrant memories crowd a heart
Peace-crowned.

Out from the world
A warmness—
Down from heaven
A blue sky;
And wherever stars gleam
O'er waters' stream.
Ships of soft-shadowed memories
Glide by.

Chicago Defender (March 16, 1929): A2.

Pagan

"I go to bed singing
And I wake up singing,"
He said.

Well, surely,
He must be a god's child
And I a pagan.
For sometimes
I go to bed

Crying.
And ofttimes
I wake up
Sobbing!

But I have one joy
He must miss—
He has no tears
For love
To wipe away!

Chicago Defender (March 23, 1929): A2.

To One Who Stayed but a Brief While

You are gone from me now—in another's arms
I see you rest; yes, without many alarms
I see you close in the embrace of my friend.
Well, why not, I ask? Isn't there an end
To all things? It was hard to let you go
For truly, I had learned to love you so!
Still, you were not for me. You knew my heart
Really belonged to another. That we should part
Was decreed from the first—we both knew.
And the days we had were really very few!
But it will be hard for me to forget
Those few brief days—a certain night. My debt
Was paid for them, never fear, another night
When I had disloyalty, love and more to fight.
Strange how one's heart can be so entangled!
Strange how a queer, green heart that dangled
From your chain lingers in my mind—other things
About you, too. Strange how one's heart brings
Such utter ecstasy and pain.

But now all this
Is past. If sometimes I remember your kiss,
No one will know. Calmly I can look upon you
In the arms of my friend—yes, a friend who
Will be kind to you—give you what I could not.
And in my heart I cannot find the least jot
Of an unkind thought against either of you.
Be happy is all I ask—and, my dear, be true!

Chicago Defender (May 3, 1930): 14.

This I Say

Now this I say: I have not felt
    Such pain as this before.
And this I say: Up to this time
    I'd not flung wide the door.

Ofttimes, I cracked it just a bit;
    Love peeked and slipped inside.
But once—but once—I let it swing
    Until it opened wide.

I need not prate of lessons learned—
    Of how, from this day on,
More care and caution I shall use.
    Admit no other one.

The fact is obvious, it seems.
    How can the door swing wide
When once it did, love came and left
    And locked it from outside.

Chicago Defender (December 19, 1931): 15.

Sonnet

Here I do sit—here do I dream of thee
Throughout the silver night so stilled and hushed,
While moon-cool beams are showered down on me,
My cheeks by fingers of the soft wind brushed.
I dream of thee whose lips are honey-dew,
Whose kisses are like nectaristic wine:
And pray the moon thy life with light imbue—
The winds that have my own lips kissed, kiss thine.
Oh loveliest, thy art my very soul—
Thou art my life and all I seek in death,
All that I ask is that thou grant this dole:
Remember me, how thou art all my breath.
Whatever may betide, may thy heart know
I think of thee, my sweet, and love thee so!

Chicago Defender (February 13, 1932): 15.

Dark Tender Eyes

They see me sit and drink my tea
    And smile and talk as others do . . .
They see a ghost; I am not here
    For I am there, somewhere, with you.

Dark tender eyes that used to be.
Do ever your thoughts wing to me?

The sullen night rears its black face;
    Fierce gusts of wind whip 'round the door.
The cold creeps in and numbs my soul—
    But I am dead; I feel no more.

Dark tender eyes that used to be.
Do ever your thoughts wing to me?

With dry and burning eyes I see
    The storm subside at last;
I hear the crackle of the fire
    That warms my room with cozy blast.

But I am cold still . . . Storms may rage
    Or utter quiet wrap the land;
There is no warming for my soul
    Unless it burns within your hand.

Life is so hopeless without you.
    I wonder how I breathe at all . . .
Yet thought of you that slays me most
    Keeps me alive to hear your call.

Dark tender eyes that used to be.
Do ever your thoughts wing to me?

Chicago Defender (February 4, 1933): 14.

I Question

What soul are you that when I see
    Your face appear to view
I must straightaway begin to talk
    Of how much I love you?

I question who you are that when
    I look deep in your eyes
My heart must quicken, throb and leap
    To unimagined skies?

What soul are you that when I see
    Your amorous red lips glow
I need but take you in my arms
    And kiss—and kiss you so?

I who have prided myself long
    On self-restraint and such,
Find now that voice and heart and lips
    Rush rampant at your touch!

My brain cries out to pierce the maze—
    To know your power complete
That you have changed one who was ice
    To flame fiercer than heat!

Chicago Defender (February 11, 1933): 14.

The First Kiss

The moon is blackened, ominous thunder rolls,
The silence of the night is cleft apart.
While frightened mortals guard their sin-sick souls,
I lie at peace, with you against my heart.
For Fate has led me to your arms at last
And I have felt your fervid mouth on mine.
With giant limbs we overstepped the past
To feast ourselves together on sweet wine.
I have not known my lips to bear such thirst—
Nor, having it, that one could slake it so.
You fill my heart 'till it will surely burst
And I must die. Oh, sweet such death, I know!

Though night is sable black, pregnant with rain,
I am at peace, your mouth on mine again...

Challenge (March 1934): 37; *Triad* (1945): 36.

Challenge

Love, I adore your timid tenderness . . .
I love your soul-filled eyes, your naive way,
Your dark-hued head, your softly sweet caress,
The voiceless, lilting things you sometime say.
But I am clay, my sweet, to earth hard-bound;
I cry for passion's breath hot on my cheek.
Demands I make may frighten and confound
For these are what I need and what I seek:
A burning love that deepest depths can plumb;
A love that adds and heightens inborn fire—
That leaves the breathless body tired and numb
When it has catered warmly to desire.

You are so sweet—so sweet! I love you much. . . .
But I am raging flame. Dare you to touch. . . . !

(From "Urns of Fate," an unpublished Sonnet sequence)

Challenge 1.3 (May 1935): 7; *Negro Voices* (1938): 128; *Shadowed Dreams* (2006): 234.

Between Ourselves

Let there be no ending to our love . . .
When you go, walk quietly,
Open wide the door but make no sound;
And when you turn your eyes on me at last,
Leave the door a moment wide
So I may glimpse the stars outside
And night, and the moon
Gleaming through the shedding trees . . .
(It will be autumn when you go . . .)

Then, turn softly and leave me.
I shall sleep—yes, even when you go,
I will sleep.
For fighting will have worn my strength away.

Then soon dawn will come—
And sun, and toil,
And all the things that fill the waking hours.
(Day will make me strong again . . .)
Dusk—dusk will be hard
For it was then I first looked up,
Beholding you.
But I shall call on all my newborn strength . . .

And when once more
Night settles softly on the world,
I shall look up and see you there
Against the night—
Stars about your fine, high head,
Flickered moonbeams at your back . . .

There can be no ending to our love . . .

American States Anthology (Vol. 1, 1936): 204.

Come Down, Stars

Come down, stars.
Come down close and let me touch
The frost that glistens on you there.
Come and make for me a pool of cold, white light;
Shower me with your icy beams,
Bathe me in their cooling flood . . .

Come down, stars—
But be ye hard and cold.

For it is of my love I needs must tell
And oh, my love is warm . . .
My love is as the sun at mid-day,
Is glowing as a wild fire in the night.
So be you hard and cold as ice . . .

Come down, stars, and list to me:
My love consumes me with its hungry fire
And wraps me in a red, red robe.
My love touches me with fingers tipped with flames
And leaves a smarting burn at every touch.
The mouth of my love brushes me across
And all my quivering nerves within
Become one blazing flare.
My love consumes me with its hungry fire . . .

Come down, stars—
Shower me with your icy beams,
Bathe me in their cooling flood . . .

Stars, come back!
Why do you hide behind the clouds?
Ah, my stars, but you are wise—
For even all your ice were not enough.
Hide, stars, hide . . .

American States Anthology (Vol. 1, 1936): 205.

Moment in Paradise

The hilltop was our haven,
High up above the earth.
Our heads were two among the stars,
Washed in moonglow, bathed in light.

Cool fingers of the wind ran through our hair,
Gently they caressed our cheeks . . .

Soon you spoke:

"Heaven must be this.
Heaven must be you and hilltops
And gentle winds blowing,
With the moon so near
And the stars very bright:
Heaven must be all of these
Brought together in a night.
I always feared that Paradise
Was not for me;
But now I fear this glimpse is all.
Soon we must descend the hill
And let our heaven go . . .
Oh, my dear,
This is all of heaven
We will ever know!"

The moon hung low, tangled in your hair.
Sobs were tangled in your throat
And on my breast your tears were wet . . .

Heaven was bitter sweet . . .

Negro Voices (1938): 129, 131.

Promise

Some day I shall write a poem for you
Some day, the seed you dropped
In the wilderness of my heart

Will burst, and little tendrils
Work themselves up—up
Until a new, proud plant is grown,
To rise above and put to shame all else.
And then one day, the tender bud,
Unfolding petals to the sun,
Will bless these eyes with full and radiant bloom;
And perfume never known by man—
Not here, not there, not in the far-off East—
Will permeate my life and wake in me
The words that have long dormant lain,
The spirit which will breathe on them
And make them live.
Then shall I write.
Then shall I write a poem no fire can burn away,
No flood can blur, no time can dim.
For you, who sowed the seed,
I shall write a poem
To reach through time and earth and death
To you.

And yet—not all the words that I might say,
Though I give my life to them
And pen them in my own heart's blood,
Could say enough.
Weak and futile are all words,
Though I make new ones to use,
Though the gods themselves speak greater words
Within my ears, and all the learned,
Long since gone, with spectral hands
Should guide my pen across the page.
Here within my saddened heart,
Words beat about with hopeless wings.
They fail me now, and all your life

They failed, and left me with no power
To make you know what I would have you know . . .

Now in the lonely sod your body rests,
Your eyes, your lips, your slender hands
No more shall move.
Gone with the light of an autumn day
Is all your beauty, all your grace.
Only memory sets before my eyes
Your smile, your bravery, your tears—
Your tears that never should have been . . .
A little trinket, a lock of hair,
A note that never reached its end—
Only these things, only such things remain.
Memory, and these things with your touch on them—
They will not forget.
But with them, too,
A nameless ache beyond regret lives in my heart
Because I know in your too-brief life
Words failed me then; and I, somehow—
I failed you then.

Beyond my power to see or touch,
They've carried you away;
But Beautiful and Most Dear,
You shall yet know.
When the seed you sowed has grown and bloomed,
Though I cannot speak
In voice of thunder, words of light,
I shall write a poem
To reach through time and earth and death
To you.

Negro Voices (1938): 131-33.

Requiem

If I should hear tonight that you were dead,
forsaking me and all this earthly place,
I do not think that I would bow my head
and weep wild tears into a square of lace.
I think I'd only silently arise
and step outside, then walk and walk and walk
until I found some hill that touched the skies,
long leagues away from any madd'ning talk.
High up, where the stars swarm bright, I'd disembark
my sorrow on the cool, receptive ground.
And in that quiet place, warmed by the spark
of memory, I think strength could be found
to bear my loss dry-eyed, and see the days
go by much as before—though with less praise . . .

Negro Voices (1938): 33; *Shadowed Dreams* (2006): 234.

If Ever You Should Walk Away

If ever you should walk away from me
With set, immobile face, and close the door
On all that has been ours or yet might be,
So will the door remain, and swing no more.
Its hinges shall grow rusty with disuse,
Its boards shall crack and mould with coming age;
Yet I inviolate will keep, and muse
On things here in our book, save that last page.
The dark may come and settle 'round my room,
The close scent as of musk bear down on me;
Still will I strain within the gathering gloom—

With heavy, burning eyes, will strain to see.
Until the dark descends to lift no more,
Inviolate I'll sit, and watch the door.

Ebony Rhythm (1948): 121.

One April

It's our anniversary.
I've had one drink—
Two drinks—
Three ...

On our anniversary
I had several drinks
Alone.

Ebony Rhythm (1948): 120.

Bury the Dead

A funeral is going on in this house
At this hour.
But no one knows.
Only I hear—the muffled church chimes
Fall with a wistful sadness on the air;
Only I see the ghostly mourners
March with measured step
As they go following the dead.
The heavy scent of roses,
The heady odor of gardenias
Envelop me with a cloying sweetness,
And organ notes, in a dirge

To the Beautiful Gone,
Swell and tremble, and softly fade away . . .

It was my beloved who died.
If you should chance upon one in the market-place
Who bears the body of this one I mourn,
Be not deceived. I do not lie.
My beloved is dead.
But no one sees the tears I weep
In solitude,
In the vacant privacy of my heart.

A funeral is being held in this house
At this hour.
I must hasten now
To bury the dead.

Triad (1945): 38.

Let the Book Close

Let the tale end. Let the book close.
There is no pain that can surpass
The excruciating stab of parting
Lest it be the continual turning
In a sore and tender wound
Of the knife of discontent.
So let it be.
Your eyes grown weary of my sight,
Your lips still against the fervor
Of my kiss,
Your heart singing a discordant tune
Against the beat of mine,
It is folly for the arms of me
To hold the murmuring unrest of you.

So bring the sword of parting and stab.
Let the tale end. Let the book close.

Triad (1945): 4.

Transient

Love is such a transient thing:
Dust upon a bird's bright wing,
Sudden raindrops in the Spring.
Love is such a *transient* thing!

Love I've cherished, lackaday—
Gave my soul unto its sway,
Believed it lasting for aye and aye.
Love, I've cherished, lackaday!

But now I've grown so terribly wise—
Seeing love with open eyes,
Stilling heart's impassioned cries.
I have grown so *terribly* wise!

Spring will soon come back again.
Love will call down every lane.
Can my wisdom stand the strain?
(Love is such a *transient* thing!)

Triad (1945): 42.

One Day

She will forget you one day, never fear.
And when you call, she'll fling the door and say
"Oh, how nice to see you, my dear!
Do come in a while. Are you well today?

And will you have a drink?"
You will sense the nonchalance in her voice—
How she must have forgot you once were more than life;
But then you will recall she had no choice.
There was no thing she could do but wield the knife
That cut the binding strings; and from the brink
Step back, and start her life once more anew.
She will remember this, if you remind—
But what will doing that accomplish you?
A sentimental mood will have made you wind
Your uncertain way to her—not sure, not clear,
Not knowing what, if anything, you hoped to see.
A sense of something decent in your heart
Will make you understand what had to be,
And you will stand, and once more you will part.
Yes, she will forget. Let her, my dear.

Triad (1945): 45.

Strange Ways

Lovers may meet and lovers may part;
Forgotten, eventually, all their days.
Others may come, and others may go—
Lives merging, then going separate ways.
This is the way things in life ever are:
A yesterday, today and tomorrow;
And what has been yesterday may not be today,
And none from the future may borrow.
But a thing which is said can never come back;
A touch which is touched ever stays;
A kiss which is kissed leaves its mark on the lips . . .
These, also, are among life's strange ways.

Triad (1945): 50.

I Offer You Wine

I offer you wine.
Ah, but my friend,
Sip it ever so slowly—
Taste the fine flavor,
Scent the bouquet.
It is wine you'll not find
In many a day.

This is the wine of me,
Pressed from my soul
By the weight of hard loneliness,
Cold like a stone,
Weighted and heavy against my heart.
It was drained through my lifeblood
Through the long, empty days,
Crushed on the treadmill
All the nights without end.

I offer you wine.
Enjoy it, my friend.

        ENGLAND
        1945

Triad (1945): 51.

Once Upon a Time

Once upon a time I was in love . . .
No, not once, but several upon-a-times!
I smile now to think
How utterly I gave myself away
To belong only to my beloved.

There were birds singing and bells ringing,
And exquisite pain, and ecstasy
That kept my breath at bay.
(Do people still love in such an abandoned way?)

Oh, it was a long ago . . .
For some time now I've been free.
It filled a need, a need now quiet.
I cherish memories of those days;
On long evenings it is pleasant to reminisce
And give them due praise.
But no pity for me, I implore.
I could not stand the bells ringing now,
Nor the birds in every tree,
Nor the agony and ecstasy as before.

I am so glad at last to be free
And to belong only to me!

Southwest Wave (Los Angeles) (December 30, 1971): 13.

Friendship

For her senior portrait in the 1920 New Trier High School yearbook, Lucia Pitts chose the inscription, "Friendship is eternal." Toward the end of her life, in October 1971, she proclaimed, "I'm grateful for friends who walk with me / Down the roads of every season." The following six poems explore two of her enduring passions: spirituality and friendship.

Satisfaction

Just a book and a song and a blazoning fire.
    And a place that I may call home.

With the cheering presence of those I love
    And who would care to roam?

Just work to do, and that with a will
    And comfort in money's stead;
When my work is done and the shadows fall.
    Just a place to lay my head.

Just water to drink and a crust or two,
    And the sun shining over the hill;
Just the stars and the moon in the dark of the night.
    And faith in His good will.

Just these simple things, and a friend or two—
    What more could man desire?
A house and a book, and lovely food
    And a friend by a glowing fire.

Chicago Defender (May 30, 1925): A12.

Friendship

This poem was untitled and published as two separate poems, each beginning with the line "I had a friend."

I had a friend
Who was clean and square;
Who was open and frank
And loving and fair.

There's nothing I'd not do
For that kind of friend.
You've my heart and my life
From beginning to end.

I had a friend
Who was always about;
But she heard wrong of me
And began to doubt.

Now the kind of friend
Who is prone to doubt
Is the kind of friend
I can do without.

Chicago Defender (June 4, 1927): A2; *Chicago Defender* (June 11, 1927): A2.

Letters

Every now and then one gets lonely—
    Now and then, perhaps, a little blue;
Every now and then one's throat chokes up a bit
    And one wonders—wonders what to do.

Oh, there are times when even sunsets
    Are veiled behind tear-misted eyes;
And there are days when even springtime
    Dips its beauty in a pit of sighs.

Then the winds of chance blow down at one's feet
    A little square from someone you know—
In it a glorious sea—a maze of words—
    With pathos, laughter and love aglow.

Or even yet, the heart may be glad—
    Nothing in life going wrong;
Then that lovely little square drops down
    And keeps the heart singing its song.

God, how they help—those little squares!
    Letters from folk who care—
They're blessings in disguise—salve for the soul—
    And they make every day wondrous fair.

Chicago Defender (May 12, 1928): A2.

To an Exuberant One

About people, two illusions have I—
Having seen them both live and die.
Not that so many years have weighted me;
Only that succeeding years made me see

So much clearer—oh, so much more keenly
That all of us are stripped of our queenly
Virtues. Through eyes strangely opened, I see.
And illusion gives way to reality.

From the tender dreams once I spun
Of such fine stuff—I turn to shun
And laugh. Bitterness mars its sound,
And I should turn to tears but that I've found

A lilting few, who in some blessed measure,
Give me back faith in the dreams I treasure
To you, especially, exuberant friend,
Whose joy in living seems without end,

I pen these lines. What a flaming light
You set in this dull place of dark night!
You come and tarry but a short while,
Yet everything is altered by your clean smile!

I should almost call you Sir Galahad.
What is it that keeps you always so glad?
Whence comes your courage—your sheer delight
In the finer things that most of us fight?

Whatever it is, oh, exuberant one,
Never lose it! May life's drowsing sun
Find it in your eyes and in your heart,
As that sun did at its journey's start.

Chicago Defender (April 19, 1930): 14.

Fly the Wide Sky

Come, friend,
Do not hold back for being afraid.
Calculate the worth; count up the cost.
Yes, that you must, and pay the cost, too.
But do not hold back for being afraid!

Will you decline the rose because it may prick,
The day's light because for an instant it is blinding?
Dig deep in your core for courage and strength.
It is there, awaiting your finding.
Confidently then, face whatever may come
And pay for the worth you find in it—
Pay for the rose with the thorn, for love with its pain;
Pay for the barrenness of an hour
For the wonder of a minute.

Do not hold back for being afraid!
"Weeping may endure for a night,
But joy cometh in the morning."
When one earns heaven by fighting through hell,
Heaven fills the heart so much more!

And peace is a thing which most happily comes
After the war which came before.

Isn't the soul in you worth its too-brief NOW?
In a life of tranquility, behind a closed door,
Tranquility is too little; a growing space is too small
On one spot of floor.

The world is your world!
Your spirit finds no fulfillment
Imprisoned in a tight-shut pod.
Only in rising and going forth, in stretching our wings,
Can we soar, soar high enough to reach God.
Do not hold back for being afraid.
Who stands cowed by fear trades the living for the dead.

Southside Journal (Los Angeles) (May 25, 1971): 20.

Cockeyed Optimist

The world is in an awful mess
And problems everywhere abound.
I know we're under strain and stress
And elusive peace cannot be found.
(The evidence will not let me doubt it
And I should be quite serious about it.)

But please forgive me if I say
This cannot plunge me into gloom.
I still love the dawn of every day
And sunlight spreading through my room.
I cannot help but bless each flower
That brightens up the world's décor
And thank the good Lord for the power
To see stars, hear music, and walk my floor.

I'm grateful for friends who walk with me
Down the roads of every season,
For people who are brave when needs must be
Even if to be they see no reason.
I cannot quench unquenchable hope
And see us lost upon this earth.
However much we err and grope,
In us there is much of wondrous worth.

But stay!
From the world's ills I've not really digressed;
Of the prophets of doom I am well aware.
But I consider mankind greatly blessed
With the mind and heart to make earth fair.

(The evidence will not let me doubt it
And I am quite serious about it!)

Southwest News (Los Angeles) (October 21, 1971): 16.

The Circle of Life

The panoply of poems in this grouping survey human life in all its richness, from youth to old age, from birth to death.

Arrival

The Regiment of Youth is treading on
    To conqueror worlds ahead;
The Heart of Youth is reaching out
    For things unnamed, unsaid.

The Heart of Youth in this new day,
    Painted—pampered and wild—

Is but the shell of stanch hearts and brave,
    Seeking better things to beguile.

New day shall dawn for this glad Youth—
    Faith, sincerity and heartsease
Will lift them up and bear them on
    To the heart's eternal peace.

They but await—the Regiment of Youth
    Whom you call sinful and low;
And, blundering, shall their own selves find
    In that day. We wait, for we know!

Chicago Defender (August 1, 1925): 22.

Similes

A plaintive cry
In the still of the night,
From the lips of a suckling child;
But mother's breast
Soothes again to rest
And the babe becomes comforted and mild.

A poignant prayer
From a burdened soul
In a world of grief and black night;
But the Father hears:
He comforts and cheers.
The dear God. He makes all things right.

Chicago Defender (May 7, 1927): A2.

Birthdays

Birthdays
Are clean, white stones—
Milestones
On the long path
To the end
Of the rainbow.
Sometimes
The sun dips down
To the purple horizon
And darkness comes,
Blotting out the day,
Before we find
The pot of gold.
How many milestones
Before the day's end
For me?

(Note: Wire your congressman and demand that January 17th be made a national holiday! It's my birthday.—T. L. C. L.)

Chicago Defender (January 14, 1928): A2.

Dirge

The days crawl by in listless apathy—
They that have passed lie in dull heaps
About me;
No scintillating shining thing
To point them out—
To set them out from all the other
Deathly tranquil days of life.
I gaze about me in sad dismay,

Viewing the listless lot of them—
The bitter lot of them.
What have they done for me?
What have they brought me?
A doleful lament to sing at dawn—
A dirge to sing at eventide.

Chicago Defender (November 3, 1928): A2.

I Have Heard Songs

I have heard soldiers sing of the poppies
That grow in Flanders fields;
I have heard men sing of God
And so have I. And now in spring
Others are singing of blue skies and love
And the exultant pain it brings.
So it is well, for every soul
Has its song, and the tune
Is not always the same.
Another song have I
And this day it is of a lonely grave
That lies out there
Beneath the wind and rain.
Once it was a happy song,
For out of the womb of her who lies
Under that resisting sod came I—
Blood of hers, and of her own flesh.
But the song ends
In a note that flings itself
Against Fate, and breaks—
A note that falls in tears.

Out there in a lonely grave
My mother lies,

Under boisterous wind and stinging rain.
Out there she lies, where nerveless hands
Thrust her tired body when at last
She came to road's end.
But only her broken body—
In the arms of Omnipotence rests her soul—
In the heart of me lives her picture,
Tender, never fading, unforgotten.
In the heart of me lives your picture.
Mother!

Chicago Defender (June 1, 1929): A2.

Nil Sacre

"No food," quoth he,
"Though nectar it may be,
Is set before thine eyes
By pure hands of the gods.
For this is earth,
Where gods walk not
But men must walk instead.
Upon thy food men's hands are set;
And though you know it not,
Men share with thee thy food.
The enemy, as other men,
Hath quaffed the cup you crave
And break the bread you love.
For this is earth . . ."

Chicago Defender (April 27, 1935): 14.

This Is My Vow

This I have made my sacred vow:
The god of bitterness shall never be my god.
Whatever is, or was, or is to be,
When I go down to death, to greet the sod,
I'll go with a taste in my mouth
Of the wine of very heaven.
The bitter cup the jaded Life need never give,
For I shall never drink—never while I live.

The sweeter draught I take for mine.
The cup of life, when first we sip, has little taste
But may, upon our whims as years go by,
Be filled with sweetest wine or bitter waste.
I have known pain and misery
But that I swear I will forget,
Remembering only hours that made the happy years:
I will not spoil my piquant wine with bitter tears.

I shall pluck moments from the days
As I would pluck the loveliest flowers from their bed.
These I will keep for my remembering—
Forgetting fingers that the thorns have bled.
Love and beauty, these will I hold,
And dancing hours, with music in my ears.
This is my vow: When I go down at last to death,
Who leans near me will catch the sweetness of my breath.

Negro Voices (1938): 133–34; *Shadowed Dreams* (2006): 235.

From the Heart

There are things in life that hurt
But have no relationship to pain...
There are things which make me love this life
With a love that aches—
Forgetful of the agonies of soul and pain of body
That wedge themselves between,
Viewing death with a disturbed, heart-breaking despair.
For what life can offer more than this?

A luminous moon rising over the gold-touched tablelands,
Quietly dispelling the dark of the night...
A picture of the still woods at dusk,
With snow settling on the waiting ground
And in the outstretched, hungry branches of the trees...
The purple shadows on the mountainside at twilight,
The sun spilling vivid rainbow colors
Over the far horizon, around the mountain slopes....

What can life after death offer to surpass
The ecstasy of a supreme moment in a beloved's arms,
His mouth caressing your own...
Or a walk down the lanes of fragrant spring,
Wordless, but hand speaking eloquently to hand...
A sail in a boat, a ride down a long winding road,
With the wind blowing against your face
In a fresh and exhilarating rush—
Or the mad magnificence of a clamorous storm...
The simple acts of common men—
A moment of meeting, with joy unhidden,
A time of parting, and tears unbidden—
A simple handclasp, the touch on your arm
Of a friend...

What better is there in any life
Than a crackling log fire on an autumn eve,
And a cozy arm-chair to dream in?
The smell of piquant and subtle perfumes,
The glory of a perfect flower—
A deep red rose opening its petals to drink in life,
A gardenia pure white, petals outstretched . . .
Good books, tall drinks and friends around;
Silences; the upliftance of quiet churches,
The sun streaming through sacred vestry windows . . .
Candle-light, and its subdued glow on the face
Of a well-beloved . . .
Quiet, clear streams come upon suddenly
By a long, hot road—
Lovely words in a song, in a poem,
In just a small speech,
Spoken in the voice of an adored one . . .
Music—beautiful music
Welling up from a throat filled with song,
In the wailing of a sad and passionate violin,
In the melody of piano keys, the resonance of an organ . . .
Oh, there are these and so many more that I love—
That fall on my heart and press and hurt
With an exquisite ache
That has no relationship to pain . . .

Dear God, if end they must, some day,
Crowd my lingering days, my now pulsing heart
With much of these and all their aching loveliness—
Forgive me that they mean so much,
Remembering it is Your hand which is the maker
Of all beautiful and lovely things—
The things that bless, and burn, and hurt. . . .

     Lucia Mae Pitts, WAC Sec., SCU 1922

Apache Sentinel (June 30, 1944): 4.

Weeds in My Garden

I have brought my sins and weaknesses out
    And looked them in the eye.
I've stared at them so very long
    I'll know them 'till I die.

They are not fair to look upon;
    And that is why, I dare say,
We seldom bring them out to face.
    But hide them all away.

I must confess I've no real idea
    What I can do with mine.
They spring like weeds among the flowers—
    Like sour grapes on the vine.

I've cut my weeds and pulled them up,
    To make my garden fair;
But in no time at all, it seems, I turn
    And find them all still there.

Despairing, I conclude at last
    They never will be killed.
All I can do is plant more flowers
    'Till my garden is so filled

With radiant blooms and fine perfumes,
    No one will see the weeds;
That they may find themselves outdone
    And bring forth no more seeds.

This is a compromise, I know—
    But still, a forward move.

I wonder if it will suffice
   And if God will approve . . .

Triad (1945): 37.

And Now Irrevocably

Now comes the time of Autumn.
In the doorway of her life she stands
And gazes with unseeing eyes upon her world.

The slow, promising beginning
Came with Spring and its halcyon days,
With her expectant wandering
Down beckoning, never-before-known roads—
The search for the lanes where the most lush
And delectable sweets might be found,
The planting and the waiting for growing,
With the eager reaching out and testing for choosing,
And happy inebriation under Spring's perfume-laden boughs,
When nothing was so good
As to be loved and sheltered by others more wise,
And never to have a care.

So the days moved gently on,
Merging one into the other,
Urged by the tender pushing of a fragrant breeze,
Until imperceptibly, Summer had come.
The promise became a question
And a deciding between this road and that,
A questing for this thing admired,
A renouncement of that thing abhorred,
And a firm resolve to gather in
The things of her desire,
Now ripened and succulent on the green bough.

And that which was good
Was to know her desires,
To have the courage to seek them out,
The agility to leap all barriers in the path.

Now comes the time of Autumn.
The things of her choosing are gathered in
With the harvest—
But not those of her desire.
The path of her decision bore
A beautiful promise, a bitter fulfillment.
Now the bewilderment and frustration,
The dismay and desperation in her heart
Speak out:
Will she be able to salvage logs for her fire
To keep winter's cold from her heart—
Food in the near barren Fall of her year
To feed her persistent, unsatisfied hunger?

For the season of planting and gathering is past,
And now, irrevocably, comes the Autumn time . . .

Triad (1945): 52–53.

Never, Never, Never

For ever and ever and ever,
  Beyond time and space,
  Never, never, never
  Will peace know my face . . .

My soul has torment for its daily bread;
For calm my heart seeks out turmoil instead.
I find cave-depths for my lonely abode
And furnish my home in confusion's mode.

From my depths I beg of a distant star
A ladder of hope to climb where they are;
But the stairs they offer fade out in mid-air—
My arms will not reach to the sky from there.

I plead to the sun when day comes at last
And my struggles with distant stars are past;
But on sun-stairs I meet only flame and burn
And so to my depths, exhausted, return.

> *For ever and ever and ever,*
> *Beyond time and space,*
> *Never, never, never*
> *Will peace know my face . . .*

Ebony Rhythm (1948): 120–21.

Time

Time is growing older
But I am not.
I view its pell-mell pace
As an insidious plot.
But it will not work, Time;
You cannot cower me.
When I face you thus spiritedly
You will have to flee
Or we'll lock in mortal combat
Over who'll drag when in this race.
And you might as well give in, Time;
I'll travel at my own pace.
There's too much yet I have to do,
Too much I have to see.
If I kept up with your rapid pace
These would be denied me.

You could match your pace with mine
And we could pause for breath.
Why should we rush so headlong
To the arms of waiting death?
But if you must rush to grow older,
I still will not.
I am defiant—yes, I am.
That for you and your plot!

Southside Journal (Los Angeles) (July 1, 1971): 7.

No Time for Tears

Life is an impatient wench.
When in the course of the day's persistent prodding
I would pause a little while
To wipe the mist from my dimming eyes,
The better to see my way,
She will have none of it.
Grumbling, she urges me on and on
To the pressing business of living.
"There is no time for the silly business of tears;
Life must be lived, not wept," she says.

But in the dead of night
Life also pauses and catches her breath.
And in that brief moment
Spanning the ended day and restless dawn,
I weep my tears.
I weep my silly tears and let them fall
Into a deep abyss of nothingness.
Then I dry my eyes, push up my chin,
So to give no sign;
So to be ready and not keep Life waiting

When the day is upon me again.
Life is an impatient wench!

Southwest News (Los Angeles) (September 2, 1971): 14.

Art

Lucia Pitts was a born writer and a multitalented artist. These poems, on the creation and appreciation of art, shed light on her aesthetic taste and admiration of beauty.

To Lights and Shadows

A soft light on the darkness,
Dim shadows on the light;
A softening of sharpness—
The reader's great delight—
   Lights and Shadows!

The column of brightness,
Of humor and song;
One place with doors open
Where welcome rings long—
   Lights and Shadows!

To Dewey R.—greetings!
The Defender I salute!
And here's to the column
Of renown and repute—
   Lights and Shadows!

Chicago Defender (August 20, 1927): A2.

Decision

I shall not sing of love so much—
    It's foolish—awfully so.
The world will think I know no else
    And rate me very low.

I can sing of other things—
    Indeed—I really can.
I'm not so awfully wrapped up
    In the genus they call man.

I guess I'll write of the Darwin theory
    Or, perhaps, of politics—
Just to change my line: but you know
    Such scribbling never sticks.

Oh, pshaw! There's no use fooling you—
    After all, I shall not change.
If I did, at this late date,
    You'd merely call me strange.

Chicago Defender (October 13, 1928): A2.

Something of Beauty

Something of beauty lies dormant
    Within my body's soul,
Covered with the dust of living
    A life that takes its toll—
A life that offers gold which
    Examined is but brass;
That swallows up the lives of men
    In one unending mass.

I've searched for words and juggled words
    To wake this sleeping thing—
To make it rise and stretch itself—
    To find its voice and sing.
But every day dust settles down
    Upon it more and more
Till now I search, know it there,
    But scarce can find the door.

That opens where I may go in and see
    Years pass; dust never stops—
My throat is rough and dry with it.
    Hope fades; ambition drops—
I despair of finding it again
    Still in my soul is the beautiful thing.
Sometimes in its sleep it stirs a bit.
    Shall I ever wake it and make it sing?

Chicago Defender (April 26, 1930): 14.

That Lady Called Lou

Dear Dewey R.:
    Let it never be said
    By living or dead
    That The Lady Called Lou
    Ever failed to come through.
    Let lasers know, near and far,
    I still occasionally twang my guitar
    But am so involved in the nation's work
    It seems as if I have to shirk
    The poetic muse and L. A. S.
    For all this heavy business.
    That is the reason for this rime
    Which takes no prize of any kind.

P.S. To be more explicit, I have that rare thing—a job—as secretary to one Dr. Clark Foreman in the U. S. department of the interior, Washington, D.C.

Chicago Defender (February 24, 1934): 14.

Warwick Castle

The Avon flows twice 'round through old Warwick's ground,
And a turbulent falls rushes down past the Mound.
The grass is quite green, the hedges shaped and clean,
And from Ethelfreda's Mound the vision can be seen
Of gay peacocks strutting and preening their tails,
Of forests, and the winding and rustic old trails
Where moonlight once brought history's lovers to woo . . .
(And oh, I wanted to share it with you!)

History's pages were opened and spread for me wide
And the spirits of the famous paraded in pride.
The years were undaunted in the turreted castle walls,
Whispering of knighthood that flowered in these halls . . .
Here invaders stormed the ramparts and arrows split the air;
Here the gallant men inside drew the invaders to their lair
While the bright bugles blew and ladies sought to hide
And men went to their death fighting valiantly outside.

I stood and remembered, and in dreams scented the musk
Of the gowns of fine ladies when they slipped out at dusk
For a rendezvous away from the fashionable crowd
With a lover in doublets, handsome and proud.
And I touched Warwick's Vase, of an old Grecian day,
Remembering Elizabeth in the grasp of love's way.
And now the wine of memories it keeps in its hold—
Standing awesome and vast, beautiful but now cold.

As I gazed and I walked where the ancients had before,
And felt myself caught up in the wonder and the lore,
My heart was both lifted and weighted down, too—
For oh, I wanted to share it with you!

>> ENGLAND
>> MAY 1945

Triad (1945): 43–44.

Poets

Pity us, the poets.
Poor fools, it is ours
To sing and to dream,
Fumbling with the stars
And the sheen of the moon—
Ever fashioning words
Into flaming phrases
The world may not read—
Being afraid, no doubt,
Their star points will pierce the mind,
Their flame burn the heart . . .

Ebony Rhythm (1948): 122.

Punctuation Suite (Eleven Parts)

In December 1945, Lucia Pitts joined her friends Tomi Carolyn Tinsley and Helen Harris in coauthoring a book of poems, which they titled *Triad*. Harris contributed twenty-eight poems, Tinsley twenty-five, and Pitts twenty-six. Dr. Nathaniel P. Tillman, Chair of Atlanta University's English Department, reviewed *Triad* for *Opportunity* magazine. He concludes his review, noting that "Miss Pitts's contributions end with 'Punctuation Suite,' a poetic orchestration that leaves no doubt of her ability as a poet."

Capitals

THE DOOR SWUNG SLOWLY ON ITS HINGE
AND I HUNG BACK TO CHAT A BIT
WITH SOMEONE PASSING BY.
AT LAST I TURNED TO CLOSE THE LEDGE—
AND THERE WERE YOU!
YOU RAISED YOUR EYES BUT ONE BRIEF TIME,
YET WHEN I LEFT THAT ROOM
I KNEW...

LONG MINUTES PASSED...
THEN ALL AT ONCE YOU LOOKED ABOUT,
SHINING WONDER IN YOUR EYES,
AS IF YOU FELT A PRESENCE NEAR.
THOUGH LONG AGO HAD DIED THE SOUND
MY FOOTFALL MADE UPON THE STAIRS,
IT WAS MY PRESENCE THAT YOU FELT...
THAT GENTLE BREEZE UPON YOUR CHEEKS,
THAT WAS MY KISS.
AND WHEN YOUR HAND FLEW TO YOUR BREAST,
IT WAS NOT PAIN THAT SOUGHT YOUR HEART
BELOVED, IT WAS I—
I!

(A capital is used as the initial letter of the first word of a sentence...)

Triad (1945): 55.

Exclamation Mark

Rush, winds!
Rush to the ends of all this earth...
Shout, thunder—

Shout out with all your awful might!
Proclaim throughout this bridled world
I have at last emerged from night!

Shine, sun—
Shine brightly down on all below . . .
Gleam, moon—
And cover earth with silver light.
My broken chains my jailers show—
I have at last escaped from night!

Life, behold—
Behold my eyes at last can see!
Death, beware—
Come when you will, with all your fright;
I crouch no more in fear and dark.
I am at last released from night—
For love is here, and holds a light!

(An exclamation mark is used after an . . . expression of an exclamatory nature . . .)

Triad (1945): 56.

Dash

—But you have heard all this before
From lips more lovely far than mine—
In voices whose alluring cadence
Haunts your vagrant heart 'til now.
All praise is now a common thing,
So long has it rained down on you;
Love has been a sea engulfing you.
How do I dare, so small I am,
To pit my voice against all this?

The song of one small stream, they say,
Which steadily flows on day unto day,
May make itself at long last heard
Above the clamoring, insistent beat
Of every other sound.

It may yet be
That you will hear my little song
And, wearied of such rearing sounds,
Find comfort in its quiet peace.

(The dash is used to mark ... an unexpected turn of the thought.)

Triad (1945): 57.

Question Mark

I wish I knew what lies behind
Your changing eyes.
And though I stare and think,
And think and stare,
It never is quite clear to me
What slumbers and awakens there,
What thoughts are born within your mind—
What things are they that touch your heart
Or stir the fires within your blood.
Your eyes reflect the stars at times,
But while I gaze adoringly,
Bewitched by all their blinding light,
So suddenly the picture shifts—
And darkness, brooding, sullen, cold,
Flows from out your half-closed lids ...
A chilling dark from which I run
And crouch in fear away from you.
And as your eyes, so are your acts ...

I wish I knew—
But still my brain, all weary, turns,
And without ceasing turns and turns,
Nor ever does it find its rest.
Tell me—tell me then, I ask—
What things are there behind your eyes;
What things live there within your heart?

(A question mark is used at the end of a direct question . . .)

Triad (1945): 58.

Italics

*I shall be thunder to crash your calm to bits
If ever you regret me.
And I shall be lightning to strike at your heart
If ever you forget me . . .*

I shall be kind and sweet and good and true—
A docile, willing slave to worship you,
So long as you love me at all.
All things I will do to merit your pride;
My life I will give you to use and to guide,
And I'll answer your faintest call.

*But I shall be thunder to shatter your peace
If ever you regret me;
And I shall be lightning to pierce through your heart,
If ever you forget me . . .*

(Italicize words to which it is desired to give emphasis.)

"Declaration," in *Negro Voices* (1938): 128–29; *Triad* (1945): 59.

Colon

It was in some older age
That we knew another world
Of loud, discordant sounds.
Now the hilltop was our haven,
High up above the earth,
And on our hilltop all was still . . .
Our heads were two among the stars,
Washed in moonglow, bathed in light.
Cool fingers of the wind ran through our hair,
Gently they caressed our cheeks . . .
Tranquility drew us in its arms,
Peace closed in about us . . .

And then you spoke:

(Before a formal quotation a colon is used . . .)

Triad (1945): 60.

Quotation Marks

"Heaven must be this.
Heaven must be you and hilltops
And a gentle wind blowing,
With the moon so low
And the stars so bright.
Heaven must be all of these
Brought together in a night.
I always feared
That paradise was not for me;
And how I fear this glimpse is all.
For soon we must descend the hill

And let our heaven go.
Oh, my dear, this is all of heaven
We will ever know!"

The moon hung low, tangled in your hair,
Sobs were tangled in your throat
And on my breast your tears were wet.

Heaven was bitter-sweet . . .

(Quotation marks enclose a formal quotation . . .)

Triad (1945): 61.

Semi-Colon

There was once I dreaded of a love so rare
It could not reek of lowly earth,
But floated as the clouds overhead
In some fair heaven all its own.
I dreamed of lush, green-covered fields
Where love and I strolled, hand in hand,
And flowers grew in bright array,
Their heady sweet scent lulling us
In quiescence so divine
That pain could never reach nor harm.
The days brought ever bright blue skies—
No sultry storms to desecrate.
Paradise was a dismal place
Compared to the world of my wistful dreams.

I have grown sadly older now.
I know that love is but an opiate
And nowhere is there long escape
From earth and earthy care.

I know that heaven is but a moment
You and I may share . . .

(Two or more sentences in which the relation in thought is very
close . . . are separated by the semi-colon . . .)

Triad (1945): 62.

Comma

On the breast of the sighing leaves
The night-wind breathes a sobbing song—
A threnody to break this heart . . .
Great clouds that move in dull grey swirls
Across the darkened, sullen sky,
Now hide securely from my eyes
The radiant moon of yesternight;
And all the stars that seemed so close
(We even counted them one while)
Recede to inky blackness far away . . .

Oh, my heart,
Remember now the light you knew—
For see, the world is dark again . . .

(Contrasted words or phrases are set off by a comma . . .)

Triad (1945): 63.

Apostrophe

Let's quiet ourselves, rebellious heart.
What matter to you and me
That love and I must so soon part?

For ours eternally
   Are all love's precious moments—
   The things that once were said,
   The moon we claimed as partners,
   The grass we made our bed.
   The fire of his mouth upon my own,
   The touch of my hand on his brow,
   Will be as much ours in time to come
   As they are here and now.

Let's quiet ourselves, my aching heart.
What matter if parting must be?
Some things are ours, and ours alone,
For all eternity.

(The use of an apostrophe indicates possession . . .)

Triad (1945): 64.

Period

Night
   Day
Poems
   Songs
Work
   Play
Rights
   Wrongs
Joys
   Fears
Plans
   Schemes
Smiles

    Tears
Hopes
    Dreams

All things we knew
Together, we two.
    Enchanting the blend
    My Lover; no regrets at
        the end.

(A period marks the end of a sentence.)

Triad (1945): 65.

APPENDIX: FAMILY TREES

Poet Lucia Mae Pitts (1904–73) was the child of Jarrett Thomas Pitts (1861–1920) and Janie Harris Pitts (1867–1926). As young women, Janie and her sister Katie moved from Alabama to Rome, Georgia, where they met and married their spouses: Janie wed Jarrett Pitts and Katie married Isaac Ernest; the couples then migrated together to Chattanooga, Tennessee. Janie and Lucia subsequently moved to Chicago, and Katie and her daughter Rozelle to Cleveland. In the book we discuss four generations of this accomplished family. To assist the reader in keeping track of so many individuals and relationships, we have compiled a genealogical chart for Lucia Pitts's maternal relatives.

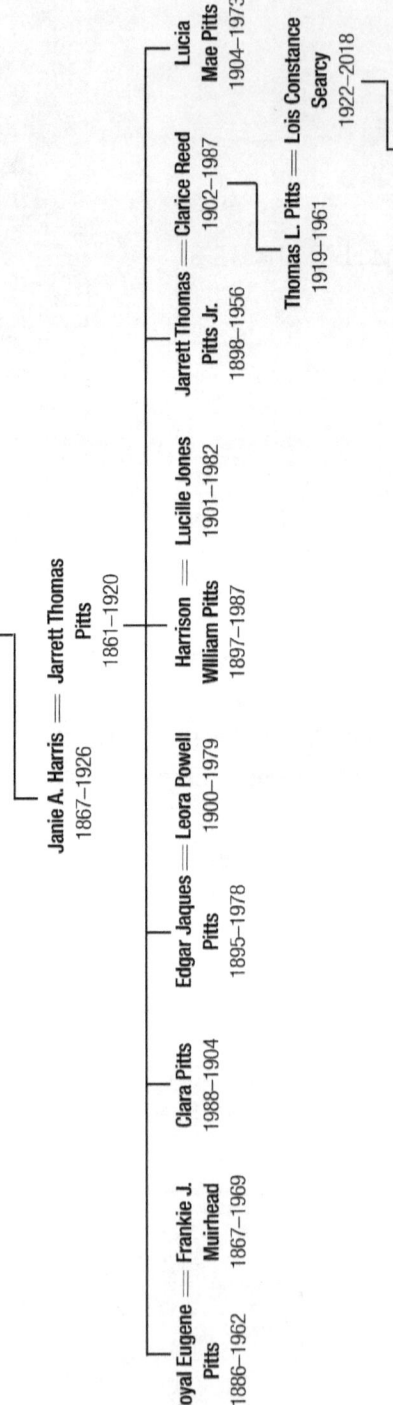

Harris–Ernest Family

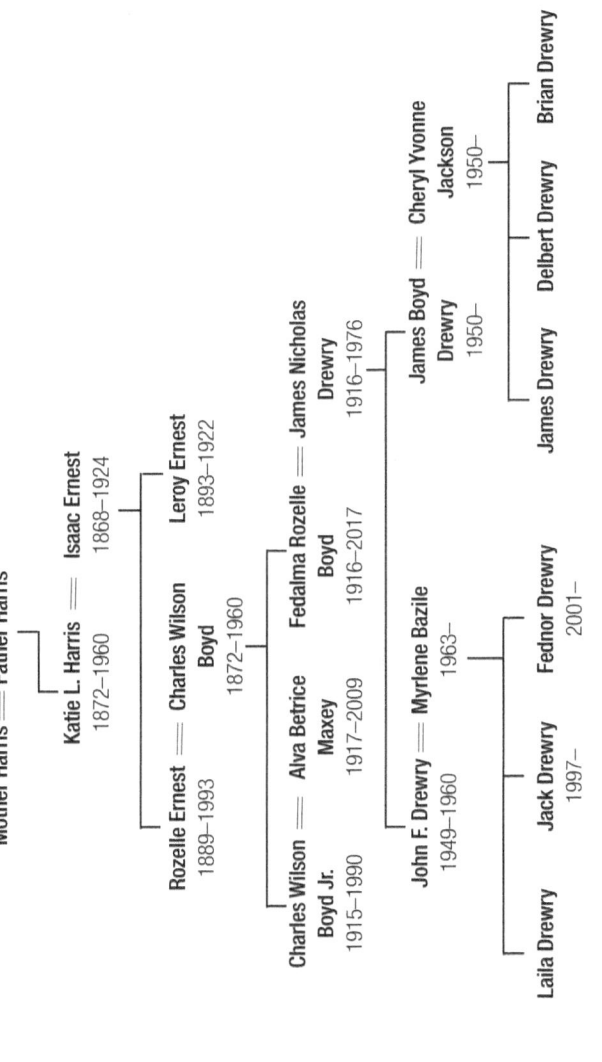

SELECTED BIBLIOGRAPHY

Aison, Gerta, ed. *American States Anthology.* Vol. 1. New York: Galleon Press, 1936.
Bell-Scott, Patricia. *The Firebrand and the First Lady: Portrait of a Friendship—Pauli Murray, Eleanor Roosevelt, and the Struggle for Social Justice.* New York: Knopf, 2016.
Burger, John S. "Annabel Carey-Prescott: African American Educator and Chicago Leader." *Journal of the Illinois State Historical Society* 112.2 (2019): 187–210.
Dagg, Anne Innis. *Mary Quayle Innis: The Woman Who Inspired Me.* Self-published: Otter Press, 2021.
Davis, Angela Y. *Blues Legacies and Black Feminism: Gertrude "Ma" Rainey, Bessie Smith, and Billie Holiday.* New York: Vintage, 1999.
Davis, Frank Marshall. *Livin' the Blues: Memoirs of a Black Journalist and Poet.* Edited by John Edgar Tidwell. Madison: University of Wisconsin Press, 1993.
Davis, Frank Marshall. "Poetry by Eighty-Three Colored Writers [A Review of *Negro Voices*, ed. Beatrice M. Murphy]." *Dayton Forum,* December 9, 1938.
Earley, Charity Adams. *One Woman's Army: A Black Officer Remembers the WAC.* College Station: Texas A&M University Press, 1989.
Ege, Samantha. "The Curious Case of 'Naughty Little Nora,' a Jazz Age Shape Shifter." *New York Times,* November 17, 2024, arts section, 6–7.
Ege, Samantha. *South Side Impresarios: How Race Women Transformed Chicago's Classical Music Scene.* Urbana: University of Illinois Press, 2024.
Foreman, Clark. "Decade of Hope." *Phylon* 12.2 (1951): 137–50.
Goldsby, Cecilia. "Orientation Notes from a Listener's Notebook." *Apache Sentinel,* July 21, 1944, 5.
Goldsby, Cecilia. "Soldiers Will Be Gentlemen If Met Half Way." *Apache Sentinel,* September 15, 1944, 4.
Harris, Helen C., Lucia Mae Pitts, and Tomi Carolyn Tinsley. *Triad: Poems.* Washington, DC: Plymouth Press, 1945.
Hill, Walter B., Jr. "Finding Place for the Negro." *Prologue* magazine 37.1 (2005).
Honey, Maureen. *Bitter Fruit: African American Women in World War II.* Columbia: University of Missouri Press, 1999.

Honey, Maureen, ed. *Shadowed Dreams: Women's Poetry of the Harlem Renaissance*. New Brunswick, NJ: Rutgers University Press, 2006.

Mitchell, Verner D., and Cynthia Davis, eds. *Dorthy West: Where the Wild Grape Grows, Selected Writings, 1930–1950*. Amherst: University of Massachusetts Press, 2005.

Monroe, Harriet. *A Poet's Life: Seventy Years in a Changing World*. New York: MacMillan, 1938.

Monroe, Harriet, ed. *Poetry: A Magazine of Verse*. Published in Chicago, 1912–36.

Moore, Brenda L. *To Serve My Country, To Serve My Race: The Story of the Only African American WACs Stationed Overseas During World War II*. New York: NYU Press, 1996.

Mullenbach, Cheryl. *Double Victory: How African American Women Broke Race and Gender Barriers to Help Win World War II*. Chicago: Chicago Review Press, 2013.

Murphy, Beatrice M., ed. *Ebony Rhythm: An Anthology of Contemporary Negro Verse*. New York: Exposition Press, 1948.

Murphy, Beatrice M., ed. *Negro Voices: An Anthology of Contemporary Verse*. New York: Henry Harrison, 1938.

Peretz, Pauline. *A Black Army: Fort Huachuca, Arizona, 1941–1945*. Translated by Arianne Dorval. New York: Cambridge University Press, 2025. English translation of *Une armée noire: Fort Huachuca, Arizona (1941–1945)*, Éditions du Seuil, 2022.

Pitts, Lucia M. "Around the U.S. in 38 Days." *Washington Afro-American*, magazine section, August 24, 1954, 1, 6.

Pitts, Lucia M. "The Back Streets of Business." *Pittsburgh Courier*, June 9, 1934, 8.

Pitts, Lucia M. "Job Holders Have Chance to Break Down Prejudice." *Pittsburgh Courier*, January 31, 1942, 9.

Pitts, Lucia M. Letter to Horace Mann Bond, February 21, 1933. Horace Mann Bond Papers, Box 15, Folder 196, Special Collections and University Archives, University of Massachusetts Amherst.

Pitts, Lucia M. *The Little Fire and How It Grew*. [1963]. State Historical Society of Wisconsin, 1981. Microfilm.

Pitts, Lucia M. "The Negro Marches On: A Brief Accounting of the Achievements in Chosen Fields of a Few Modern Negroes." May 9, 1935. Dewey Roscoe Jones Papers, Box 7, Folder 10, Vivian Harsh Research Collection, Chicago Public Library.

Pitts, Lucia M. "Written for Women." *Chicago Defender*, January 31, 1942, 15.

Putney, Martha S. *When the Nation Was in Need: Blacks in the Women's Army Corps During WWII*. Lanham, MD: Scarecrow Press, 1992.

Roundtree, Dovey Johnson, and Katie McCabe. *Mighty Justice: My Life in Civil Rights*. Chapel Hill, NC: Algonquin, 2019.

Stovall, Mary E. "*The Chicago Defender* in the Progressive Era." *Illinois Historical Journal* 83.3 (1990): 159–72.

Treadwell, Mattie E. *The Women's Army Corps: United States Army in World War II*. Washington, DC: GPO, 1954; reprint St. John's Press, 2016.

Wall, Cheryl A. "Nora Holt: New Negro Composer and Jazz Age Goddess." In *Women and Migration: Responses in Art and History*, edited by Deborah Willis, Ellyn Toscano, and Kalia Brooks Nelson. Cambridge: Open Book, 2019.

Watts, Jill. *The Black Cabinet: The Untold Story of African Americans and Politics During the Age of Roosevelt*. New York: Grove Press, 2020.

West, Dorothy. *The Richer, the Poorer: Stories, Sketches and Reminiscences*. New York: Anchor Books, 1995.

INDEX

Abbott, Robert S., 1
Adams, Charity, 14, 39–40, 71
Adams, George C., 20
Adventure magazine, 24
Aison, Gerta, 32
Allison, Alice, 67
All Souls Unitarian Church, 43–44
"All That I Ask," 10
Alpha Kappa Alpha sorority, 15, 17, 44
American Negro Exposition, 35, 47
American States Anthology, 32
Apache Sentinel, 36, 66, 92
"Apostrophe," 47
Arizona Daily Star, 42
Army of the United States, 87
Askins, Violet, 64
Associated Negro Press, 33
Auls, Novella, 41–43, 58n124, 67

"Back Streets of Business, The" (essay), 34
Baker, Jesse N., 20
Barrett, Elizabeth. *See* Long, Elizabeth Barrett
Barrett, Sarah, 12
Bennett, Gwendolyn, 2
Bethune, Mary McLeod, 38, 45, 86
Bland, Consuelo, 67

Blues Legacies and Black Feminism (Davis), 9
Bond, Horace Mann, 29; friendship with, 20–21; helping to publish *Urns of Fate*, 22
Bond, Julian, 21
Bond, Norma Elizabeth, 44
Bontemps, Arna, 29, 35
Bousfield, Midion O., 67
Boyd, Charles Wilson, Jr., 15, 47–48
Boyd, Julia, 44
Boyd, Sharkey, 44
Branch, Phyllis, 67
Breath in the Whirlwind (LaMarre), 51
"Brief Song," 10, 20
Brooks, Gwendolyn, 4–5, 6, 53n3
Burger, John, 5
Burton, Edna, 67
Burton, John, 28–29
Bynner, Witter, 6, 7

Caroling Dusk (Cullen), 29
Cartwright, Charlotte, 67
"Challenge," 7, 9, 32
Challenge magazine, 28, 32
Chicago Commercial Institute, 5, 20
Chicago Defender, 1–2; Brooks's role in, 6; editing, 4, 6, 23–24; "Lights and

Chicago Defender (continued)
    Shadows" poetry column in, 1, 2, 19, 23–24
Chicago's Black World's Fair. *See* American Negro Exposition
Chicago Whip, 22
Choicy Du Bac, 81–82
Cleveland, Rev. James, 17
"Cockeyed Optimist," 52
Cole, Nat King, 25
Coleman, Anita Scott, 29, 30, 53n3
Coleman, Bessie, 17
Colored Woman in a White World, A (Terrell), 47
"Confession," 7, 9
Crisis, The, 7
Cullen, Countee, 7, 22, 28, 29, 53n3
Cuney, Waring, 2

"Daring Me to Forget," 24
Daughters of the American Revolution (DAR), 32
Davies, Arthur Powell, 43–44
Davis, Angela, 9–10
Davis, Frank Marshall, 10, 22, 24, 29, 53n3; praising Pitts's love poetry, 30; review of *Negro Voices*, 29
"Decision," 11
Dedeaux, Olive, 67
Denniston, Arabella, 45
Detroit Times, 15
Dibble, Eugene H., Jr., 20
Dizikes, John, 50
Drewry, John F., 48
Du Bois, W. E. B., 27

Ebony Rhythm (Murphy), 47
Edward, Glenn, 67
Ege, Samantha, 3
Eliot, T. S., 6
Ellington, Duke, 25, 27, 35
Ernest, Katie, 12, 48
Ernest, Rozelle, 12, 15, 48
Eva Jessye choir, 57n87

"Fallen Castles," 19
"First Kiss, The," 47

Fishel, Leslie, 50
Flaming Letters, 58n124
"Fly the Wide Sky," 48
Follies Bergere, 80, 86
Foreman, Clark, 28, 31, 33
"Forest at Dusk," 30
Fort Des Moines, Iowa, 36, 63–64
Fort Huachuca, Arizona, 3, 36–38, 42, 51, 64–65
Fowler-Shaver, Lillian, 18, 22
Franklin, Aretha, 17, 25
"Franklin Delano Roosevelt," 32
Frost, Robert, 6

Gates, Mildred, 67
Gillisslee, Marie B., 67
Goldsby, Cecilia, 22–23
Gordon, Edythe Mae, 29
Green Pastures, The (Connelly), 27
Gregg, Arthur J., 39

Handy, W. C., 8, 28
Haney, Della, 67
Hardy, Edwin N., 65, 66–67
Harlem (Thurman), 27
Harlem literati, 28
Harlem Renaissance, 2, 12, 27
Harmony Quartet, 8, 18
Harris, Helen C., 46–47, 167
Harrison, Richard B., 27, 34
Haygood, William, 50
Holt, Nora, 2, 3, 4; influence on Pitts's poetry, 10; musical philosophy, 8–9
Hopkins, Pauline, 13
Horne, Frank, 44
Horne, Lena, 25, 38
Huff, William Henry, 10
Hughes, Langston, 2, 7, 28, 35, 53n3, 66
Huston, Zora Neale, 28
Hymel, Kevin, 40

Ickes, Anna Wilmarth, 26–28
Ickes, Harold L., 26, 28, 32, 43, 44
"I Have Heard Songs," 18, 25
"I'll Sing My Songs," 24–25
Innis, Mary Quayle, 5
"I Shall Come to Thee," 19

Jackson, Mahalia, 17
Jacobs, Ruth Sarver, 41–42, 87
Johnson, Corienne Robinson, 22, 33, 44
Johnson, Eugene Harper, 67
Johnson, Helene, 2, 30
Johnson, James Weldon, 29, 34
Jones, Dewey Roscoe, 20–21, 22, 31
Just, Bernice, 44

Kellum, David, 22
King, Martin Luther, Jr., 17
"Kiss, The," 32
Knopf, Blanche, 4

"Lady Called Lou, The" (TLCL). *See* Pitts, Lucia M.
LaMarre, Hazel Washington, 51
Langston, Irving Y., 12–13
LASers, 2, 23
LaVigne, Gertrude Cruse, 42–43
"Letters," 31
"Let Them Come to Us," 35, 47
"Lights and Shadows" poetry column, 1, 2, 19; editing, 23–24
Lindsay, Vachel, 4
Little Fire and How It Grew, The (autobiography), 1, 4, 22, 44
Livin' the Blues (Davis), 24
Long, Alonzo G., 12–13
Long, Elizabeth Barrett, 12–13
"Love Song of J. Alfred Prufrock, The" (Eliot), 6

Marian Anderson Protest Committee, 32
Marshall, Thurgood, 27
Martin, Evelyn C., 67
Millay, Edna St. Vincent, 4, 6, 7, 10
Mills, Harry, 67
"Moment in Paradise," 30
Monroe, Harriet, 6–7, 24
Moore, Brenda L., 14, 41
Muirhead, Frankie J., 14, 15
Murphy, Beatrice, 28, 47; advocating inclusion of unknown Black poets, 29; editorial board formation, 29
Music and Poetry magazine, 8

National Association of Negro Musicians (NANM), 8–9
National Bar Association, 20
National Defense Advisory Commission (NDAC), 35
"Negro, The" (essay), 34
Negro, The (script), 66–67
"Negro Marches On, The" (essay), 33–34
"Negro Mother, The" (Hughes), 37, 66
"Negro Speaks of Rivers, The" (Hughes), 7
Negro Voices (Murphy), 29, 47
New Trier High School, 5–6, 20, 27, 52
Nugent, Bruce, 28

Officer Candidate School (OCS), 67
"Once Upon a Time," 51, 53
One Negro WAC's Story (memoir), 51, 58n124; basic training, 63–64; at Choicy Du Bac, 81–82; decision to join WAC, 61–64; discharge from WAC, 81, 85–86; first Negro WACs departing for overseas duty, 69–70; Fort Huachuca assignment, 64–65; intensive training, 67–69; postwar updates on battalion, 86–87; reflections on military service, 85–86; return journey from Europe, 81–85; service in England, 70–76; service in France, 77–80; 6888th Central Postal Directory's duty, 71–72; V-E Day celebration, 76; volunteering for overseas duty, 66–68; WAC third anniversary celebration, 76–77; writing and staging *The Negro* script, 66–67
Opportunity magazine, 7, 47
Outer Guard, 32, 33

"Pagan," 25
Palmore, Lil, 16
"Period," 47
Peterson, Mildred, 67
Pilgrim Baptist Church, Chicago, 17, 56n46
Pinkey, Lloyd, 67
Pitts, Edgar Jaques (Lucia's brother), 12, 27, 53; education, 14–15; military service, 13–14; opposition to Lucia's WAC enlistment, 14; work and marriage life, 15–16

Index

Pitts, Harrison William (Lucia's brother), 8, 12, 13–16, 53
Pitts, Janie A. Harris (Lucia's mother), 5–6, 12, 14–15, 30; death, 25; role in Pilgrim Baptist Temple, 17–18
Pitts, Jarrett (Ralph), Jr. (Lucia's brother), 12, 13, 16
Pitts, Jarrett Thomas (Lucia's father), 12, 13
Pitts, Lucia M., 1–3; autobiography rejection, 50–51; "Black Cabinet" membership, 28–35; and Gwendolyn Brooks, 4–5, 6; Chicago life, 13–14, 22–23; church involvement, 17, 43–44; Company B friends, 41–43; death, 53; and Dewey Jones, 31; education, 5–6, 14–15; employing Black women, 32–33; employment, 2–3, 10, 14, 19–20, 25–28, 35–36, 44–45; essays, 33–34; family and early life, 3, 12–19, 47–48; Great Depression impact, 25; and Horace Mann Bond, 20–21; influences, 6–7, 18–19; "Lights and Shadows" poetry column, 23–24; "The Lady Called Lou" pseudonym, 21; literary networks, 4, 6–8; love poetry, 4, 7–11, 30; and music, 8–10, 16–18; origins, 11–12; Outer Guard foundation, 32, 33; as panelist with "women writers of the district," 47; poetic interests, 28–29, 30–31, 35, 37, 51–52; poetic style, 9, 10, 52–53; post-war life, 43–53; publishing books, 6, 22, 29–30; racial discrimination, 26; recognition, 10–11, 32; retirement, 49–50; and Richard Harrison, 27; Roosevelt's death, 32; Sabalala, relationship with, 24–25; solo cross-country road trip, 48–49; theater engagement, 22; *Triad* book of poems contribution, 46–47; volunteer services, 45. See also *One Negro WAC's Story*; 6888th Central Postal Directory Battalion; Women's Army Corp
Pitts, Lucille W. (Lucia's half-sister), 12–13, 15, 49, 53
Pitts, Royal Eugene (Lucia's brother), 12; education of, 14–15; illness, 63–64;
military service, 13; opposition to Lucia's WAC enlistment, 14, 62
Pitts, Thomas LaVerne (Lucia's nephew), 16–17, 38, 79, 92
Pittsburgh Courier, 26, 34
Pitts Pub, 16
Poetry magazine, 6
Poole, Elva, 67
"Portraiture" (Coleman), 30
Pound, Ezra, 6
Powell, Adam Clayton, Jr., 34, 38
Powell, Leora, 15–16
Primitive, The (Himes), 50
"Promise," 30
"Prove It on Me Blues" (Rainey), 18
Pryor, L. Dorothea, 17–18, 22
"Punctuation Suite," 47, 167

"Raid, The" (Sabalala), 6
Rainey, Gertrude "Ma," 4, 8; contrast with Pitts, 10; female sexual autonomy and love, 19; romantic relationship with Smith, 18–19
"Recuerdo" (Millay), 7–8
Regal Theater (Bronzeville, Chicago), 22, 25
Reid, Dorothy Louise, 67
"Requiem," 30
Robinson, Corienne Kathleen, 32–33, 44, 57n92
Roosevelt, Eleanor, 38, 76
Roosevelt, Franklin Delano, 75–76; NDAC creation, 35; Pitts in "Black Cabinet," 2, 32
Roundtree, Dovey Johnson, 45; about beauty vs. injustice, 46
Roundtree, William, 46

Sabalala, Santie, 6, 24–25
Sandburg, Carl, 6
Savoy Ballroom, 22, 25
Sebree, Charles, 34
"Semi-Colon," 47
sexuality, 8–9; in Lucia's "Confession," 19; in Rainey's lyrics, 19
Silence, The (LaMarre), 51

Silver Birch Club, 72
Simpson, Grace, 67
6888th Central Postal Directory Battalion, 35–43, 71–72, 85; Congressional Gold Medal, 39–40; LaMarre's service, 51; portrayal in popular culture, 40; role in, 31, 39, 41, 43, 61. See also *One Negro WAC's Story;* Women's Army Corp
Six Triple Eight, The (Perry), 40
Small, Pauline, 67
Small Fire and How It Grew, The (autobiography), 50–51
Smith, Bessie, 2, 4, 8, 9; contrast with Pitts, 10; romantic partnership with Rainey, 18–19
State Emergency Relief Administration (SERA), 15–16
Staupers, Mabel Keaton, 38
St. Edmund's Episcopal Church, Chicago, 14, 16–17
Street in Bronzeville, A (Brooks), 5
Sunset Café, 25

Talbert, Fannie, 67
Terrell, Mary Church, 47
Terrell, Robert, 47
"This Is My Vow," 30, 52
Thurman, Wallace, 2, 27–28
Tinsley, Tomi Carolyn, 28, 46, 167
"To an Admirer," 7, 9, 19
"To Lights and Shadows," 1, 2
Tolson, Melvin, 35
"To My Flowers," 51
Tonkins, Vashti B., 41, 81
"Trees at Night" (Johnson), 30
Triad (Pitts, Tinsley, and Harris), 46–47, 167; review, 47, 167

Universal Negro Improvement Association, 26
Urns of Fate (sonnet series), 22

Van Vechten, Carl, 4
Vincent, J. J., 65–66

WAC. *See* Women's Army Corp
"WAC Speaks to a Soldier, A," 31, 37, 53, 66
Walker, Maggie L., 34
Wallace, Babe, 67
Washington Afro-American, 3, 49
"Weary Blues, The" (Hughes), 7
Weaver, Robert C., 33–35
Wendell Phillips High School, 5
Whisonant, Lawrene, 67
Women's Army Corp (WAC), 61, 86, 87; basic training, 63; decision to join, 62–63; Dovey Johnson Roundtree's role in, 45–46; Fort Huachuca assignment, 64–66; intensive training, 38–39, 67–69; living conditions and daily life, 71–72, 78–79; Pitts's enlistment and service in, 14, 36–38, 40–41, 45, 62–63; overseas deployment, 67–71; recreational activities and cultural interactions, 72–74, 76; third anniversary celebration, 76–77; tragic deaths in France, 40; "WACs Pick Pin-Up" article, 38. *See also* 6888th Central Postal Directory Battalion; *One Negro WAC's Story*
"Writing on Poetry" column (LaMarre), 51
"Written for Women," 33
WWII History magazine, 40
Xenia Daily Gazette, 13
Your Legacy from Thaddeus Stevens (Boyd), 47–48

THE BLACK SOLDIER IN WAR AND SOCIETY
New Narratives and Critical Perspectives

―――――――――

A Soldier's Life: A Black Woman's Rise from Army Brat to
Six Triple Eight Champion
EDNA W. CUMMINGS

Race, Politics, and Reconstruction: The First Cadets at Old West Point
RORY MCGOVERN AND RONALD G. MACHOIAN, EDITORS

www.ingramcontent.com/pod-product-compliance
Lightning Source LLC
Chambersburg PA
CBHW030855170426

43193CB00009BA/617